Berlitz

BOLOGNA
POCKET GUIDE

 **Walking Eye**
mobile app

Discover the world's best destinations with the Insight Guides Walking Eye app, available to download for free in the App Store and Google Play.

The container app provides easy access to fantastic free content on events and activities taking place in your current location or chosen destination, with the possibility of booking, as well as the regularly-updated Insight Guides travel blog: Inspire Me. In addition, you can purchase curated, premium destination guides through the app, which feature local highlights, hotel, bar, restaurant and shopping listings, an A to Z of practical information and more. Or purchase and download Insight Guides eBooks straight to your device.

TOP 10 ATTRACTIONS

SANTO STEFANO
Enchanting complex of medieval churches, cloisters and crypts. See page 47.

LE DUE TORRI
The Two Towers are celebrated symbols of the city. Climb to the top of Torre degli Asinelli for splendid views. See page 42.

MAMBO
A sleek modern Arts Centre, with a fashionable café. See page 66.

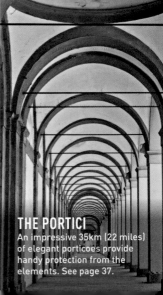

THE PORTICI
An impressive 35km (22 miles) of elegant porticoes provide handy protection from the elements. See page 37.

GASTRONOMY
Indulge in Bologna's culinary delights and find out why they call the city 'La Grassa' (The Fat). See pages 91 and 100.

NEPTUNE'S FOUNTAIN
Giambologna's show-stopping bronze of Neptune in the heart of the city. See page 30.

SAN LUCA
Climb the world's longest portico to the hilltop sanctuary church of San Luca. See page 72.

PALAZZO DELL'ARCHIGINNASIO
Former university building with Anatomical Theatre where human corpses were dissected. See page 38.

BASILICA DI SAN PETRONIO
The monumental basilica ranks among the most imposing of Italy's Gothic churches. See page 34.

PINACOTECA NAZIONALE
The city's finest art collection with works by Bolognese and other Italian masters. See page 57.

A PERFECT DAY

9am

Breakfast
Kick off the day with coffee and diet-busting brioches at the Caffè Sette Chiese on Piazza Santo Stefano. Secure a seat under the arches of the portico for fine views of Santo Stefano church.

10am

Strada Maggiore
From Via Santo Stefano take the Corte Isolani, a quaint medieval warren of galleries and cafés, to Strada Maggiore, lined with porticoes and palazzi. Browse in elegant antique shops and/or visit the delightful Museum of Music and Gothic Church of Santa Maria della Vita.

Noon

Culinary delights
Plunge into the maze of medieval alleys off Piazza Maggiore with tantalising delis, fresh food stalls and a chic covered food hall. For lunch grab a *piadina* (sandwich) crammed with Parma Ham, Mortadella and local cheeses, or head for Tamburini at Via Caprarie 1, a famous gourmet deli and café.

11am

Historic core
Head for Piazza del Nettuno, host to Giambologna's celebrated statue of Neptune, and beyond to Piazza Maggiore, which is overlooked by the Basilica di San Petronio. Here, absorb everyday life in this sweeping square, then take a peek inside the monumental interior of San Petronio.

2pm

Ancient university
Take elegant Via dell'Archiginnasio and visit the frescoed Palazzo dell'Archiginnasio, first seat of Bologna's university and where, in the Teatro Anatomico, some of the earliest dissections in Europe were performed. Have coffee and cake at Zanarini, an upmarket café on Piazza Galvani.

IN BOLOGNA

3pm

Leaning towers

Head northeast to the Due Torri and gawp at the tipsy towers. Offload a few calories by taking the 480 steps to the top of Torre degli Asinelli. Wander around the nearby former Jewish Ghetto, now home to some delightful artisan workshops.

8pm

Trusty trattoria

Close by, dine on fabulous Bolognese pasta (made on the spot as you will see) at Dal Biassanot, Via Piella. Beside the restaurant take a peek through the Finestrella (little window) di Via Piella over the canal and you might believe you were in Venice.

4pm

University quarter

Wander along Via Zamboni for a flavour of the university. Pass noble palaces converted to bustling faculties, bohemian bars, eclectic cafés and arty bookshops.

6pm

Aperitivo time

Head to Le Stanze, the private chapel of the Palazzo Bentivoglio at Via del Borgo di San Pietro 1, for a unique combination of cocktails and 16th-century frescoes.

10pm

Jazz in the cellar

Listen to the best live jazz in Bologna at Cantina Bentivoglio, Via Mascarella 4/B, in the antique cellars of the Palazzo Bentivoglio.

CONTENTS

INTRODUCTION

Capital of Emilia Romagna, arguably the most civilised region of Italy, Bologna is renowned for its university, its cuisine and its traditional left-wing stance. Hence the oft-quoted sobriquets: Bologna 'La Dotta' (the Learned), Bologna 'La Grassa' (the Fat), and Bologna 'La Rossa' (the Red). The city is also famous for its beautifully preserved historic centre, and La Rossa refers as much to the rich red of its palaces, towers and porticoes as it does to its left-leaning politics.

Located on the edge of the Po Plain at the foot of the Apennines, the city is a fine example of Roman and medieval town planning, with its ancient town gates, radial plan and long straight streets. It stands on the Via Emilia, the arrow-straight road laid down by the Romans from Rimini to Piacenza. In the Middle Ages this was where Europe's first university was established, and a town quickly grew around it. Dozens of towers rose above the city, built both as watchtowers and as status symbols by the succession of dynasties that ruled Bologna until it became part of the papal states in 1506. The city prospered from its setting, surrounded by fertile plains and vineyards which supplied its convivial inns. Within its walls, urban life was more liberal than in most other provincial cities and a free-thinking entrepreneurial people flourished. Today Bologna is a progressive modern city with a vibrant student population, thriving professional and business sectors and a buzzing street life.

BOLOGNA LA GRASSA

Of the three sobriquets Bologna is perhaps best known globally as 'La Grassa', a reference to its rich culinary tradition. Prosperous Emilia Romagna is the legendary bread basket of Italy, a region which has given birth to culinary delights such as *prosciutto crudo* (Parma ham), Parmesan cheese and world-renowned balsamic vinegar. Emilian cuisine reaches its height in Bologna which is widely acclaimed as the culinary capital of Italy. It is famed for fragrant pink Mortadella, *ragù* (the real Bolognese meat sauce) but above all else for egg pasta. *Tortellini* alone would be a good enough reason to visit

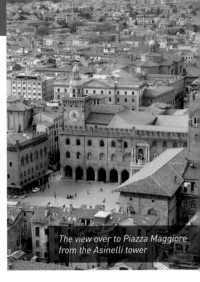

The view over to Piazza Maggiore from the Asinelli tower

Bologna. Legends abound as to the pasta's origins, one of which gives credit to a young cook of a wealthy Bolognese merchant who modelled the pasta on the perfect navel of his master's wife – which even if apocryphal, says much about the seductiveness of the cuisine. *Sfogline* (pasta ladies) in trattorias or pasta shops can still be seen rolling out sheets of pasta and cutting out the tiny delicate shapes. Flourishing pasta cookery schools (there are 25 in the city) and the annual pasta-making competition, *Il Matterello d'Oro* (The Golden Rolling Pin), are further evidence that the home-made *tortellini* is in good shape.

A stroll through the teeming medieval streets of the central Mercato di Mezzo reveals tantalising food stores and market stalls brimming with gleaming fresh produce. Gourmet delis are crammed with whole hanging hams and great wheels of cheese, enticing passers-by to stop for a few slices of wafer-thin *prosciutto*, washed down perhaps with a cool glass of

Perfect pasta

The Bolognesi take their food very seriously. In 1972 the Accademia Italiana della Cucina (Academy of Italian Cuisine) decreed that the exact width of a cooked strand of *tagliatelle* must be 1/1,270th of the height of the Asinelli tower, 9mm (0.3 in).

Pignoletto. When it comes to restaurants it's not so much about Michelin-rosetted temples of cuisine with exotic new delicacies but earthy family-run trattorias, where the cuisine is simple and the emphasis is on perfect ingredients. While a handful of places in the city give a nod to lighter contemporary cuisine, Bologna for the most part carries on serving what it's best at, and at a leisurely pace.

CULTURAL LEGACY

The city is as passionate about culture as it is about food and enjoys a long tradition of intellectual enlightenment. The medieval lawyers, scholars and sculptors of its university paved the way for scientific breakthroughs that helped shape the modern world and it was the university that was the city's economic powerhouse. The elaborately sculpted sarcophagi of great scholars in the city's Medieval Museum give some idea of the importance attached to academia. Professors rose through the social ranks and were richly rewarded in death as well as life.

The medieval era also witnessed the rise of fine monuments, great Gothic churches rich in art and the characteristic colonnades. These elegant porticoes, now a Unesco World Heritage Site, have always provided a refuge from the elements and a meeting place for Bolognesi from all backgrounds. In times gone by they provided cover for furtive assassinations and the amorous assignments, of among others, Boccaccio and the

Marquis de Sade. Here Verdi and Rossini trampled the porticoed streets in search of inspiration, just as the late novelist Umberto Eco set out in search of material for his medieval whodunits. In the summer months musicians strike up under the arcades, artists set up easels, and all year round there is a lively café scene with tables spilling out under the porticoes, assured of shelter from rain, snow or the intense heat of the summer sun.

Thanks to the porticoes and the compact size of the historic centre, Bologna is a delightful city for strolling. There are sufficient monuments, museums and artistic treasures for several days' exploration. Many of the city's churches are rich repositories of art while Renaissance or Baroque palazzi, often embellished with frescoes, make fine settings for the city's main museums. Palazzo Poggi, seat of the university, is home to some fascinating specialist museums while the nearby Pinacoteca houses the city's finest art collection, with works by Giotto, Raphael and the great Bolognese painters. In the Baroque period the artistic output flourished here and Bologna became the pre-eminent influence in Italian painting.

A LIVING CITY

Despite its illustrious history, wealth of architecture and gastronomic reputation Bologna attracts far fewer tourists than cities

Neptune's Fountain

Colourful fresh produce

such as Florence or Venice. As a result it feels far more Italian, gritty and real and less museum-like, making an enticing alternative to these more famous cities. Fears of arid scholarship are banished by the buzz of the student area, with bohemian bars overlooking faculties tucked into frescoed palaces. Bolognesi of all ages come out for the evening *passeggiata*, the ritual stroll; there's a vibrant café and bar scene, an action-packed calendar of events with concerts, jazz, theatre and art exhibitions and a lively gay scene. In term time the population of 390,000 (over 1 million in greater Bologna) swells by around 100,000. But even during holiday time there's plenty going on and the Bè Bolognaestate festival from June to September ensures a summer of music, art and theatre. The city has a rich music heritage and has played host to the likes of Verdi, Rossini and Puccini. In 2006 it was appointed Unesco Creative City of Music, a prestigious recognition that honours the city's music tradition – as well as the lively contemporary scene.

Created on the back of agricultural wealth the regional economy has thrived for centuries but always moved with the times. Engineering is a regional strength but embraces everything from cutting-edge car manufacture to machine tools and precision robotics. Emilia Romagna is serious car country, with Ferrari, Maserati and Lamborghini all produced here. The city and the region have always been committed to making both money and desirable products, from Mortadella cured meat to Ducati motor-bikes, while not neglecting agriculture. In keeping with the city's entrepreneurial, forward-thinking approach, manufacturing and the service industries have been decentralised leaving the his-toric centre vibrant and liveable, yet well preserved.

Contemporary Bologna is not without the social challenges and high unemployment which confront other cities of Italy (the Italian youth unemployment rate stands at 33 percent at the time of writing). But this is a city that knows how to thrive, and as the capital of one of the richest regions in Europe with

⊙ A MEDIEVAL MANHATTAN

In medieval times Bologna bristled with over 100 towers. Built by Bolognese nobles these varied in height between 20 metres (65ft) and 60 metres (197ft), with rival families striving to see who could build the highest. But by the 16th century the *torri* had fallen out of fashion. Fire and the fear of collapse were con-stant hazards, and the great palazzi took over as the main sta-tus symbols of noble families. In the late 19th century, during urban regeneration, many of the surviving towers were demol-ished. Most of the remaining ones tend to tilt, often at alarming angles. Alongside the Cattedrale di San Pietro the Azzoguidi tower, also called Altabella (the Tall Beauty), is the only one standing perfectly vertical. The most famous towers however, and symbols of the city, are the Asinelli and the Garisenda, the 'Twin Towers'. You can climb 498 steps to the top of the Asinelli. Or if you fancy having a tower all to yourself book into the Torre Prendiparte (see page 139). Be warned though, the price – and the climb to the top – are not for the faint-hearted.

Inside the Palazzo d'Accursio

the third highest GDP per capita in Italy it is consistently ranked among the top Italian cities for quality of life. It looks after its cultural legacy too. Recent years have seen major restoration of monuments within the historic centre, and the opening or reopening of eight buildings, mainly churches and palaces, which have been recovered by the Fondazione Cassa di Risparmio in Bologna and now form part of a cultural itinerary. A further incentive for visitors is the city location at a major rail hub, making it the perfect springboard for day or half-day trips to the art-filled cities of Emilia Romagna. Modena, the birthplace of one Pavarotti, and the home of Maserati and Ferrari, as well as of a superlative Duomo, is a mere half-an-hour trip by train; gourmet Parma is less than an hour away. Closer to Bologna, and providing respite from the city streets in summer, are the Colli Bolognesi, the wooded hills of southern Bologna: the first foothills of the verdant Apennines.

Bologna has many facets: a city of history, expressed in every tower and portico, a city of culture and museums, musicians and artists, a top university city, a city of gastronomy and a city of business and trade. But above all this is a city where everything is harmonious, and the cult of beauty permeates most aspects of life. 'La Rossa' notwithstanding, Bologna remains a paradigm of the good life: a citadel of good taste set in the proverbial land of plenty.

A BRIEF HISTORY

Bologna's location, strategically sited between northern and central-southern Italy, has been both a curse and a blessing. The Bolognesi haven't enjoyed many centuries of peace but the various powers that coveted and ruled over the centuries left behind a heady mix of culture and riches. Despite invasions, sieges and plagues, as well as devastation in World War II, Bologna has managed to emerge as one of Italy's wealthiest and most dynamic cities. Its history goes back to a pre-Etruscan civilisation, but it is the medieval period, when a red-brick turreted town grew up around Europe's oldest university, that truly defines the city.

Carving depicting early students at the university

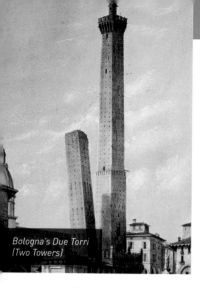
Bologna's Due Torri
(Two Towers)

EARLY SETTLERS

As the Bronze Age merged into the Iron Age in around the 9th century BC, northern and central Italy were occupied by the Villanovian civilisation, named after a site discovered at Villanova just outside Bologna in 1859. This gave way in the 6th century to an Etruscan settlement, called Felsina, on the area where Bologna is today. The town flourished as a trading centre thanks to its link to the port of Spina on the Po Delta. It was a period of peace and prosperity and by the 8th century the Etruscans were dominating the entire region. Displays in Bologna's Archaeological Museum, including grave goods, exquisite statuettes and jewellery, give an insight into the affluence and sophistication of the Etruscan culture.

At the start of the 4th century Etruscan Bologna underwent radical upheaval, with successive waves of invasions by the Celts from over the Alps. The tribes occupied large stretches of Italy, north of the Apennines and the Marches region. It was one of these tribes, the Boii, which gave the name Bononia to the settlement when it came under Roman control in 189 BC.

By this time the Romans had conquered Cisalpine Gaul and set up colonies in the fertile Po Plain. They had built the Via Flaminia, stretching from the Adriatic coast over the Apennines to Rome, and in 187 BC completed the long straight Via Aemilia

(Emilia), running from Rimini on the east coast to Piacenza, through their newly conquered territories. This established Bononia as a key centre, linking up with the Via Flaminia and hence giving direct military and trading access from Rome. The settlement was substantially rebuilt and extended and although much of Roman Bologna is overlaid by the medieval city, Roman street plans are still visible and the route of the old Via Emilia cuts right through the centre. There are also Roman remains in the Archaeological Museum and in churches where Roman capitals were recycled and incorporated into medieval columns in surprisingly harmonious ways.

HUNS, GOTHS AND LOMBARDS

In the early 5th century the region fell prey to barbaric invaders emigrating south, with invasions from Visigoths and Huns. Despite the incursions a strong Roman Christian culture prevailed. The close relationship between Ambrogio, the Archbishop of Milan, and the Bolognese Bishop, Petronius, who later became the patron saint of the city, enabled the construction of the first wall around the city and the addition of 'holy protection' in the form of four crosses set outside the walls.

Ravenna, a relatively unknown provincial town surrounded by swampland, took centre stage when Honorius, last Emperor of Rome, made it capital of the Western Roman Empire in 404. With the fall of the Western Roman Empire in 476 it came under Gothic rule, like the rest of Italy, but enjoyed a period of recovery and became a rich and powerful city, famous for its glittering early Christian and Byzantine mosaics.

The Lombard King Liutprand captured Bologna in 727. Less than 50 years later the Lombards in turn were ousted by the Franks under Charlemagne who restored the city to the papacy. The city's most ancient churches date back to this era.

COMMUNES AND DYNASTIC POWERS

The exquisite porticoes of Via Farini

In the 11th and 12th centuries Bologna succeeded in wresting itself from Ravenna, whose archbishops controlled the region. It was now free to enjoy the status of an independent commune – or free city state, thus ensuring considerable political and economic autonomy. The University of Bologna, which is now recognised as the oldest in Europe, was founded in 1088 and brought international renown to the city (see box). It was a period of major development too, with the creation of elegant porticoes and high-rise towers, built for wealthy families. Less evident today are the canals which served the watermills to power the textile industries, especially silk. The waterways were also used for ships carrying cargo as trade expanded. By 1200 Bologna had a population of around 50,000 and was one of the great cities of Europe.

But as in the rest of Italy it was also a time of factional strife. The city was one of the main cities of the Lombard League (1167), a medieval alliance of North Italian communes against Emperor Frederick I Barbarossa. There were constant struggles between the Guelphs, supporters of the free cities and the pope, and the pro-Holy Roman Empire Ghibellines. The Guelphs faught constantly with Ghibelline Modena and won a victory against them at the Battle of Fossalta in 1249. The son of Emperor Frederick

II, known as Enzo of Sardinia, was captured and imprisoned in Bologna's Palazzo di Re Enzo until his death in 1273.

Internal power struggles led to the decline of the communes and the rise of the region's great family dynasties, ranging from semi-feudal lordships to fully fledged dukedoms and courts of European renown. Throughout the 15th century Bologna was governed by the mighty Bentivoglio family, who produced five successive leaders, and introduced an enlightened regime, bringing in the printing press and embarking on a building programme.

⊙ BOLOGNA 'LA DOTTA' ('THE LEARNED')

Medieval Bologna's most significant event was the foundation of Europe's first university, believed to have been in 1088. For the first 470 or so years of its existence the university had no fixed location and lectures were held in public buildings or convent halls scattered around the city. Under Pius IV the Palazzo Archiginnasio (see page 38) was built in the city centre in 1562 and this served as the seat of the university until 1803 when it moved permanently to its present premises on Via Zamboni. The prestige of the law school made the city a European centre of scholarship which drew the finest minds of the day. Bologna also developed one of Europe's earliest medical schools and acquired a reputation for scientific research that survives to this day. Palazzo Poggi, the present-day seat of the university, is home to many of its faculties, the university library and a cluster of museums, including some fascinating scientific collections that were used for teaching in former times. The university remains one of the country's finest academic institutions and boasts some of the loveliest university buildings in the country.

Pope Clement VII and Charles V arriving in Bologna for Charles's coronation

In the region as a whole, dynastic rule was elevated to a way of life, with the noble courts becoming noted centres of culture, from the Farnese dynasty in Parma to the d'Este dukes in Ferrara, and the Malatesta lords in Rimini. During the Renaissance the ducal courts, especially that of the d'Este, became cultural and artistic centres attracting the finest artists.

CENTURIES OF PAPAL DOMINATION

Bologna's role as a prestigious centre of learning had helped make the city one of the richest, most important and densely populated in Europe. Such prosperity and independence presented a threat to papal power, so the city was annexed by the Papal States in 1506 when Pope Julius besieged Bologna. A year later, encouraged by the papacy, the Bolognesi sacked the monumental palace of the now fallen-from-favour Bentivoglios. Following Bologna, Parma and Piacenza were later annexed by the Papal

States and the papal dynasty ended one of the most enlightened Renaissance city-states when it swallowed up Ferrara in 1598 and the remains of the d'Este dukedom transferred to Modena.

The life of Bologna as part of the Papal States was to endure for almost three centuries. When Charles V was crowned Holy Roman Emperor by the pope in 1530 he chose to have the coronation in Bologna's Basilica of San Petronio. His troops had sacked Rome three years earlier and Bologna by this stage enjoyed an importance second only to the capital of the Papal States. It was a double coronation for Charles was also crowned King of Italy in the Palazzo Pubblico (now the Palazzo Comunale). The combined event was chronicled as the 'Triumph of Bologna' for the pomp and splendour of the ceremonies. The following few months saw fervent construction in the city, the papacy showcasing its power and influence through symbolic triumphal arches, classical architecture and statues.

The last decades of the 16th century saw the school of Bolognese painters flourish under the Carraccis, the family of artists who challenged the affectations of Mannerism and satisfied the desire of the Counter-Reformation for a new religious art of simplicity and clarity with a direct appeal to the emotions. Guido Reni, who trained with the Carracci, became one of the greatest painters of the 17th century. But while Bologna was a major art centre and saw the rise of new churches, monasteries and palazzi, it was otherwise a period of political and intellectual stagnation, dominated by the reactionary reforms of the Counter Reformation.

FOREIGN INTERVENTION

Papal rule was interrupted briefly with Napoleonic troops sweeping into Italy in 1796. Bologna, Ferrara, Mantua and Reggio Emilia formed the Cispadane Republic, later to be amalgamated in to the short-lived Cisalpine Republic with Milan as its capital. The French, who were welcomed in Bologna, made improvements to the city, such as the ring road outside the city walls and the transfer of the University from the Archiginnasio to Palazzo Poggi.

Under the Congress of Vienna in 1815, following the defeat of Napoleon, Bologna was returned to the Papal States. But real control of much of northern Italy rested with reactionary Austria whose troops garrisoned the city from 1815. Insurrections spread through Bologna, Modena and Parma, starting in 1831. Austrian rule finally came to an end when Camillo Cavour, the architect of Italian Unification, decided the only way of defeating Austria was with the support of France. In 1859 the troops of Vittorio Emanuele and Napoleon III of France defeated the Austrians at Magenta and Solferino. The following year the citizens of Bologna voted to become part of the Kingdom of Savoy, which was to become the Kingdom of Italy in 1861.

WORLD WAR II

The 19th century saw Bologna rehearsing its future role, as a radical socialist city in a left-leaning region within the broad 'red belt' of central Italy. Even so, the city flirted with Fascism during the period between the two world wars, and paid the price in 1943–5. The Emilian Apennines marked the Nazis' Gothic Line, making Bologna a strategic target for Allied attacks. The aerial bombardments wreaked havoc on the city, destroying or severely damaging over 40 percent of the buildings in the historic centre.

The bourgeoisie and the land-owning classes succumbed to Fascism, but during the last days of the war, partisans from the area provided the fiercest resistance to Nazi occupation.

The Bologna hinterland also suffered Italy's worst Nazi atrocity against civilians. In 1944 the Marzabotto massacre of 1,830 civilians and partisans in the Apennines, south of Bologna, spurred widespread condemnation, as did the Nazi deportation of Jews from Ferrara and Bologna.

MODERN BOLOGNA

In 1945 the city elected a Communist administration and never really looked back. The administration mutated into a left-wing coalition and over the next 50 years imposed an individualistic, modern vision on the city. Bologna became one of the first cities to show that there was no contradiction between a left-wing council and capitalism with a human face. It privatised key social services and encouraged public-private partnership. A bastion of social democracy, civil rights and communal culture, the city pioneered pedestrian precincts, conservation areas, communal housing, gay rights and affordable childcare, as well as sheltered housing for the elderly and student facilities.

But the city of good governance was not without its fair share of the turbulence in Italy during the late 1960s and 1970s. Over a decade of political crime and violent clashes culminated in the 'Bologna Massacre' on

The Civil Guard, established in Bologna in 1847

2nd August 1980, when a bomb attributed to a Fascist terrorist organisation ripped through a waiting room of Bologna's Central Station leaving 85 dead and 200 wounded. A gash in the wall and the station clock, permanently fixed at 10.25am, the exact time of the explosion, commemorate the event.

To the dismay of local leftists the long line of left-wing mayors was broken when a centre-right coalition won the elections in 1999, headed by Giorgio Guazzaloca, a conservative businessmen and President of the Chamber of Commerce. In 2004 the left came back to power and has kept it ever since. Centre-left Flavio Delbono resigned after 7 months at his post following his involvement in a corruption scandal and was replaced by Virginio Merola in 2011, who was re-elected mayor in 2016.

Bologna has a thriving industrial sector, with emphasis on engineering, electronics, machinery and automobiles. The Fiera is one of the largest exhibition centres in Europe, hosting around 30 international events annually, with themes ranging from construction and packaging to cosmetics and fashion. Like the rest of the country Bologna has suffered from the economic downturn in recent years but continues to retain its place among the top Italian cities for quality of life, wealth and welfare.

Museum of Modern Art of Bologna (MAMbo)

HISTORICAL LANDMARKS

9th century BC Villanovan civilisation emerges near Bologna.

4–5th century BC Etruscan settlements in Felsina (Bologna).

189 BC Foundation of Roman Bologna (called Bononia)

AD 402 Ravenna proclaimed capital of the Western Roman Empire.

476 Ravenna conquered, signalling the fall of the Western Roman Empire

751 End of Byzantine domination in northern Italy.

1088 Foundation of Bologna University, the oldest in Europe.

1167 Bologna joins the Lombard League, an alliance of self-governing republics to defeat Emperor Barbarossa.

1374 Bologna's city walls completed.

1460–1506 Bologna ruled by the local Bentivoglio lords.

1506 Bologna annexed by the Papal States.

1629–31 Bologna loses 15,000 citizens in the plague of 1629–31.

1797–1802 The city becomes part of the Napoleonic Cisalpine Republic.

1815 Bologna and Emilia restored to the Papal States.

1871 Italian Unification.

1915 Italy joins the World War I Allies.

1940 Italy enters World War II as an ally of Nazi Germany.

1943–5 Bologna bombed by the Allies.

1945–9 Bologna has an uninterrupted string of left-wing mayors.

1980 Fascist terror attack on Bologna Central Station, with 85 deaths.

1982 Italian football team wins World Cup in Spain.

2000 Bologna is European Capital of Culture.

2006 Bologna is named Unesco City of Music.

2010 Centre-left mayor, Flavio Delbono, resigns after involvement in corruption.

2011 Virginio Merola elected as mayor, leads a left-wing coalition.

2012 20 May: Earthquake and aftershocks in Emilia-Romagna leave 26 dead, 20,000 homeless. The Genus Bononiae cultural, artistic and museum itinerary opens in the historic centre.

2016 Celebrations mark the 900th anniversary of the founding of the city. Virginio Merola is re-elected mayor.

2019 Bologna ranks 7th out of 110 Italian cities for quality of life.

Fontana del Nettuno is a
popular meeting point

 # WHERE TO GO

Bologna is the perfect place to explore on foot. Almost all of the cultural attractions are packed into the historic centre, a large part of which is a Limited Traffic Zone, where traffic is restricted from 7am to 8pm. Furthermore the city is flat and the pavements are protected by arcades. From Piazza Maggiore and from the hub around the famous two towers, streets fan out towards the city gates and the *viali*, the circle of avenues which follows the ancient walls. Via dell'Indipendenza links the rail and bus stations to Piazza Maggiore, and at its southern end forms a T with Via Ugo Bassi running west and Via Rizzo running east. These three main arteries, which are Bologna's high streets, are completely vehicle-free at weekends.

PIAZZA MAGGIORE AND AROUND

Piazza Maggiore and its antechamber, Piazza del Nettuno, form the symbolic heart of the city, showcasing the political and religious institutions that define independent-minded Bologna. Overlooked by brick-built palazzi and the vast mass of San Petronio the sweeping Piazza Maggiore was (and to a certain extent still is) the stage setting where Bolognesi gathered for speeches, ceremonies, meetings and protests. The square is also a showcase for daily life, from Prada-clad beauties to protesting students, pot-bellied sausage-makers to perennially flirtatious pensioners. Just off the piazza the labyrinthine food market provides culinary diversion and the porticoes shelter some of the city's most exclusive shops.

The Neptune Maserati link

Motoring enthusiasts may recognise Neptune's trident in the *Fontana del Nettuno*. It was adopted by the Modena-based Maserati car company as their logo.

PIAZZA DEL NETTUNO

The focus of the piazza is *Fontana del Nettuno* ❶, the celebrated bronze fountain to Neptune sculpted by Giambologna in 1556. An Italian in all but birth (he was born Jean Boulogne in Flanders) the Mannerist sculptor spent most of his working life in Florence but it was the *Fountain of Neptune* in Bologna which made his name. The sculpture depicts a monumental, muscle-bound Neptune (nicknamed 'Il Gigante') with four *putti,* representing the winds, and four voluptuous sirens who sit astride dolphins, spouting water from their nipples. Given Bologna's turbulent relationship with the papacy, the citizens delighted in the fact that the nude Neptune was considered a profane, pagan symbol by the papal authorities. The statue caused a furore when first unveiled and a Counter-Reformation edict decreed that Neptune should be robed. But the priapic sea god is now free to frolic. (Locals take great delight in pointing out the best vantage point for viewing the god's impressive manhood).

PALAZZO RE ENZO AND PALAZZO DEL PODESTÀ

Facing the fountain, on the east side of the square, stands **Palazzo Re Enzo** (access only during exhibitions), named after the son of Emperor Frederick II, Enzo 'King of Sardinia', who was defeated at the Guelphs versus Ghibellines Battle of Fossalta in 1249 and was imprisoned here for 23 years until his death in 1272. Adjoining the palace and facing Piazza Maggiore is the elegant **Palazzo del Podestà** (access only during exhibitions), built as the political seat of power in the 13th century. It is graced by a Renaissance porticoed facade on the Piazza Maggiore side and distinguished by its 13th-century brick tower, the Torre dell'Arengo, originally built to summon citizens in case of emergency. The vault below, the Voltone del Podesta, was once occupied by terracotta statues of the town's patron saints. The attraction today is the echo in the 'whispering gallery' – face one of the four corners of the arcade and your voice will be transmitted to the opposite corner.

The wall on the west side of Piazza del Nettuno features photos of hundreds of partisans who fought for the Resistance in World War II. Of the 14,425 local partisans, including over 2,000 women, 2,059 died. Italy was liberated from Nazi domination on 21st April 1945 by which time Bologna had been devastated by aerial bombardments. A further memorial honours the victims of the bomb explosion at Bologna's main railway station in 1980 which left 85 dead and 200 wounded.

PALAZZO D'ACCURSIO

The vast and imposing building on the west side of Piazza Maggiore is the **Palazzo d'Accursio**, also known as the **Palazzo Comunale ❷** (www.musei bologna.it/arteantica; Tue–Sun 9am–6.30pm, some ceremonial halls open Tue–Sun 10am–1pm if not being used for council meetings; charge only for

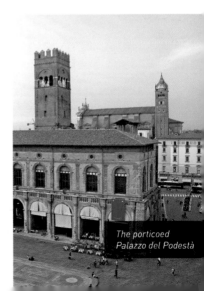

The porticoed Palazzo del Podestà

Palazzo Comunale, the medieval town hall remodelled in the Renaissance

the Collezioni Comunali d'Arte, the Municipal Art Collection). The palace dates back to the 13th century and was originally the residence of a well-known medieval lawyer, Accursius. It was later bought by the city and remodelled as an affirmation of papal authority. In 1530, two days before he was crowned Emperor in San Petronio, Charles V was crowned King of Italy in the chapel of the Palazzo d'Accursio, receiving the Iron Cross of Lombardy. A suspended passage was built especially for the occasion, linking the palace to San Petronio across Piazza Maggiore.

The huge bronze statue (1580) above the portal of the palace depicts Pope Gregory XIII, the Bolognese pope who reformed the old Roman calendar, replacing it with his own Gregorian one, still in use today. Above and to the left of the doorway is a beautiful terracotta statue of the *Virgin and Child* (1478) by the Italian sculptor Niccolò dell'Arca. Cross the courtyard and climb the magnificent corded staircases, where horses once thundered past, to the frescoed interiors on the first and second floors. Restyled by papal legates in the 16th century, the **ceremonial halls** are elaborately frescoed and have fine views over Piazza Maggiore. The Sala Rossa, or Red Room, with its huge chandeliers, is a favourite venue for civil ceremonies. The Museo Morandi which opened here in 1993 was moved to MAMbo (see page 66) in 2012 while this part of the palace was restored. The museum will return here after the work is complete. The many rooms of the **Collezioni Comunali d'Art** at the top of the palace display Emilian works of art from the 13th to 19th centuries, worth visiting for a sense of the decor, furnishings and artistic taste under papal rule, rather than for great art.

SALABORSA

Part of the monumental Palazzo Comunale complex, the **Biblioteca Salaborsa** (Mon 2.30–8pm, Tue–Fri 10am–8pm, Sat 10am–7pm; free) was built within the shell of the former Stock Exchange (Borsa). The building is now a spacious multimedia library and cultural space, designed in Art Nouveau style. A glass floor in the Covered Square reveals excavations of the medieval and Roman settlements including part of the forum and Roman pavement, and these can be accessed from the lower basement level (Mon 3–6.30pm, Tue–Sat 10am–1.30pm and 3–6.30pm; free).

Before its current role, this sizeable section of the Palazzo Comunale served diverse purposes. In 1568 the Bolognese naturalist, Ulisse Aldrovandi, founded Bologna's Botanic Garden in the courtyard here for the academic study of medicinal plants. This was one of the first botanic gardens in Europe (Bologna's botanic garden today is in the university quarter). The courtyard later became a training ground for the military, then in the 20th century served variously as bank offices, a puppet theatre and a basketball ground before becoming the Stock Exchange.

PIAZZA MAGGIORE

A sunny day is a summons to sit at café tables in the **Piazza Maggiore** ❸ or on the steps under the arcades and soak up the atmosphere. Dominating the great central square is the vast but incomplete Basilica of San Petronio, favourite church of the Bolognesi. The slightly raised platform in the middle of the piazza is familiarly called the *crescentone* after the name of the local flat bread, *crescente*, which it resembles in shape.

BASILICA DI SAN PETRONIO

Dedicated to Petronius, the city's patron saint, the 14th-century **Basilica di San Petronio** ❹ (www.basilicadisanpetronio.it; Mon–Fri 7.45am–1.30pm, 2.30–6pm, Sat–Sun 7.45am–6.30pm; church: free, terrace: charge) is the city's principal church. As one of the most monumental Gothic basilicas in Italy, the church would have been larger than St Peter's in Rome had not Pope Pius IV put a stop to construction by using the funds for the creation of a new university, the Palazzo Archiginnasio. As a consequence the facade was never completed, hence only the partial cladding in pink Verona marble and the cut-off transept which you can see down the alley to the right of the basilica. Even so, San Petronio is still monumental and remains the city's best-loved church, representing a manifestation of civic will rather than religious power. Built over Roman foundations the vaulted church reveals columns recycled from the Augustan era, which meld perfectly with medieval additions.

The highly expressive reliefs on the **Porta Magna**, the central portal, were the last great work of Sienese sculptor Jacopo della Quercia, occupying the last

> ### Bologna Welcome Card
>
> The excellent tourist office on Piazza Maggiore can supply you with a Bologna Welcome Card. At €25 for the Bologna Welcome Card Easy and €40 for the Bologna Welcome Card Plus, they are good value giving you free admission to many city museums and attractions, plus discounts for shops, restaurants and events. Also available at www.bolognawelcome.com.

San Petronio's *half-completed facade*

13 years of his life (1425–38). The architrave displays scenes from the New Testament, and on the two pilasters on either side of the door, dramatic reliefs with subjects taken from the Old Testament. Michelangelo, who visited Bologna in 1494, admired these reliefs and used several of the motifs (such as *The Creation of Adam*) for the Sistine Ceiling. The lunette features the *Madonna and Child* between St Petronius and St Ambrose.

The immense but simple interior of the basilica has witnessed historical events, not least of which was the crowning of Charles V as Holy Roman Emperor in 1530 (see page 23). Set in the floor on the left is a 17th-century sundial, measuring almost 60m (197ft) and said to be the world's biggest church sundial. It was of particular interest to travellers on the Grand Tour and today it still attracts plenty of interest, especially at noon on a sunny day when rays touch the line of the sundial. The second chapel on the left is dedicated to San Petronio and contains

Madonna and Child above the altar

the relics of the saint. The **Bolognini Chapel** (4th on the left) remains virtually intact, and has striking early 15th-century frescoes by Giovanni da Modena, depicting the *Journey of the Magi*, *the Life of St Petronius*, *Paradise* and a harrowing scene of the *Last Judgement*. There are 20 more chapels, an organ to the right of the altar, dating from 1470 and still functioning (the one opposite still works too but is relatively modern at 1596), and a museum with projects for the completion of the facade which were never carried through.

From the recently revamped **panoramic terrace** of the basilica (access from Piazza Galvani by lift and a few steps; Mon–Thu 11am–1pm, 3–6pm, Fri–Sun 10am–1pm, 2.30–6pm) there are splendid views of the cityscape and the Apennine hills to the south.

MUSEO CIVICO ARCHEOLOGICO

From Piazza Maggiore the Via Archiginnasio takes you under the porticoes past the city's most elegant shops, including the loveliest arcades, known as the Pavaglione. The **Museo Civico Archeologico** ⑤ (www.museibologna.it/archeologico; Mon and Wed–Fri 9am–6pm, Sat–Sun 10am–6.30pm; opening times may be extended during temporary exhibitions) is housed in the former hospital of Santa Maria della Morte (of Death), which was dedicated to the terminally ill. The lovely courtyard is framed by Roman statuary and leads to Giambologna's statue of Neptune which is displayed at the top of the main staircase. Bologna's early history is traced through Celtic tools, Etruscan urns, Attic vases and Classical Greek terracottas, proof that the Bolognese talent for trading dates back to its earliest history. The sheer number of exhibits – around 200,000 – in old-fashioned dimly lit galleries can be overwhelming but the museum has one of the best Etruscan collections in Italy. Two large galleries are devoted to the Etruscan civilisation in Bologna (9th–4th centuries BC), featuring terracotta and bronze ossuaries, funerary stelae with depictions of fantastic animals and exquisite terracotta askos

⊙ CITY OF PORTICOES

A distinctive feature of the city are the *portici*, or porticoes, extending almost 40km (25 miles). These graceful, tranquil arcades were originally built of wood outside shopkeepers' houses as extra space for trade. The original portico had to be a minimum of 7 'Bolognese feet' high (2.66m) to enable those on horseback to pass through. From 1568, due mainly to fire hazards, porticoes had to be made of brick or stone. A few of the old wooden ones survive and one of the best preserved examples is the lofty portico of Casa Isolani in Strada Maggiore. The Portico San Luca, running for nearly 3.5km (2 miles) up to the hilltop Sanctuary of San Luca, is the longest portico in the world. Over the centuries the porticoes have been much admired by travellers both for their architectural interest and their protection against the elements. In a city renowned for rain and snow in winter, and searing heat in mid-summer, they couldn't be more convenient.

(small vessels for pouring liquids). There are also good displays of Roman antiquities and (easy to miss) an impressive Egyptian collection in the basement.

PALAZZO DELL'ARCHIGINNASIO

Just beyond the Archaeological Museum is the cultural set-piece of the frescoed **Palazzo dell'Archiginnasio ❻**, built in 1562–3 as the first permanent seat of Europe's most ancient university (www.archiginnasio.it; Palace Courtyard and open gallery: Mon–Fri 10am–6pm, Sat 10am–7pm, Sun 10am–2pm, free; Anatomical Theatre and Stabat Mater Hall: Mon–Fri 10am–6pm, Sat 10am–7pm, Sun and hols 10am–2pm, if not occupied by events). Before the construction of the Archiginnasio the schools of law and medicine had been scattered around various venues of the city. This remained the seat of the university until 1803 when it moved to its current location in Via Zamboni. Today the palace houses the precious collection of 800,000 works of the Biblioteca Comunale (City Library), the richly decorated Sala dello Stabat Mater, a former lecture hall where Rossini's first Italian performance of *Stabat Mater* was held in 1842 under the direction of Donizetti, and the fascinating Teatro Anatomico (Anatomy Theatre).

The fine courtyard, with its double loggia, and the staircase and halls are all decorated by memorials commemorating masters of the ancient university together with around 6,000 student coats of arms. The courtyard was frequently the scene of university ceremonies, one of the most intriguing being the Preparation of the Teriaca (Theriac), a drug for animal bites and later the all-cure medicine, formulated by the Greeks in 1st century AD and concocted from fermented herbs, poisons, animal flesh, honey and numerous other ingredients.

Some of the first human dissections in Europe were performed in the **Teatro Anatomico**, shaped like an amphitheatre and adorned with wooden statues of famous university anatomists of the university and celebrated doctors. There is nothing remotely macabre about the tiered seats and professors' chair – apart from a canopy supported by depictions of a couple of skinned cadavers, *gli spellati*. The Church forbade regular sessions of dissections but when they did take place they were popular events, open to

Legendary Tamburini deli

the public. As photos at the entrance illustrate, this wing of the building was devastated during the bombardment of 1944, but was reconstructed immediately after the war, using the original wooden sculptures that were salvaged from the rubble.

The Via dell'Archiginnasio leads into **Piazza Galvani**, named after the 18th-century Bolognese scientist Luigi Galvani, pioneer of bioelectromagnetics. Through his experiments on frogs he established that bioelectric forces exist within animal tissue. The statue in the square shows Galvani gazing at a frog on a stone slab. For a break from sightseeing head to Zanarini on the corner of the Piazza, a great spot for coffee and cakes.

QUADRILATERO

The maze of alleys tucked away off Piazza Maggiore is known as the Quadrilatero. It is an ancient grid of food shops where the mood is as boisterous as it was in its medieval heyday. The ancient guilds of the city, such as goldsmiths, blacksmiths, butchers, fishmongers and furriers had their headquarters here and many of the street names today recall their trades. The market is the place for a true taste of Emilia, with open-air stalls, specialised food shops and a covered market, **Mercato di Mezzo ❼**, now transformed into a stylish food hall selling enticing regional produce and a wide range of freshly made tapas-style snacks to take away or eat in, very casually, at communal tables. From here the market spills out onto Via Drapperie, Via Clavature and Via degli Orefici. Gaze and graze is the mantra of most visitors. On offer are juicy peaches and cherries, sculpted pastries, navel-shaped handmade pasta, slivers of delicious pink Parma ham, succulent Bolognese Mortadella, still-wriggling seafood and wedges of superior 'black rind' parmesan.

By day, few people can resist lunch at **Tamburini** (Via Drapperie/Via Caprarie 1), the legendary gourmet deli with a self service, followed perhaps by a delicious pastry at **Atti** (Via

◎ WHERE TIME STANDS STILL

Only the word 'Vino' above the doorway hints that you might have arrived at an inn. The inconspicuous Osteria del Sole, just off Via Pescheria at Vicolo Ranocchi 1D (www.osteriadelsole.it) is Bologna's oldest inn, dating from 1465. It's an atmospheric, rough-and-ready spot, with old framed photos on the walls, cheap wine served by the glass and long tables for customers to bring their own food – which they have done for centuries. Pick up a picnic from the market stalls or from neighbouring delis, order your glass of Sangiovese or Pignoletto and sit with cheerful old boys playing cards, students from the university or the occasional tourist who has managed to locate this elusive inn.

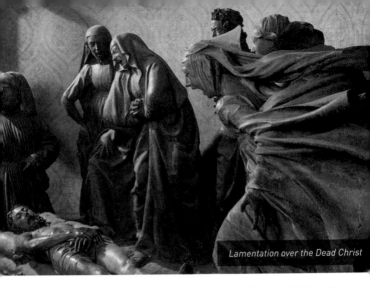

Lamentation over the Dead Christ

Drapperie 6); or a picnic of charcuterie from **Salumeria Simoni** (Via Drapperie 5/2A), where whole hams hang from the ceiling and wheels of cheeses and thick rolls of Mortadella are crammed into the windows. In the evening the Quadrilatero becomes a chic spot for an *aperitivo* in an outdoor café.

SANTA MARIA DELLA VITA

After the bustle of the surrounding market the church of **Santa Maria della Vita** ❽ (Via Clavature 8; www.genusbononiae.it; Tue–Sun 10am–7pm) is a haven of peace. Although boldly frescoed the restored Baroque interior is overshadowed by the *Lamentation over the Dead Christ* (1463) by Niccolò dell'Arca, a remarkable composition in terracotta portraying life-size grieving mourners at the death of Christ. The church was part of a religious hospital complex and it is thought that Niccolò dell'Arca may well have studied the faces of the sick and suffering to have achieved such stunning expressions of grief. The figure of Nicodemus is traditionally described as a self-portrait. In the oratory, where temporary exhibitions are held, there is another poignant lament in terracotta, the *Death of the Virgin*, by Alfonso Lombardi.

EAST OF PIAZZA MAGGIORE

With its long rows of noble palazzi and secret courtyards, the east side of the medieval city has always been the most fashionable quarter of the city. The Strada Maggiore follows the route of the Roman Via Emilia which linked with the Via Flaminia – the route to Rome. The porticoed street is lined by a succession of senatorial palazzi which once belonged to ruling families. To the north, Via San Vitale was formerly called Via Salaria, for it was along here that salt was transported into the city from the Cervia salt flats south of Ravenna. Via Santo Stefano, the ancient road to Tuscany, is flanked by yet more fine mansions and leads to, and beyond, the beguiling complex of Santo Stefano.

DUE TORRI

Dominating Piazza di Porta Ravegnana, site of the main gate of the Roman walls, are the **Due Torri ⑨**, the Two Towers. The **Torre**

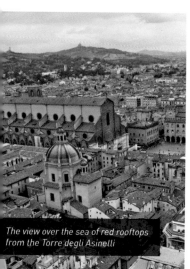

The view over the sea of red rooftops from the Torre degli Asinelli

degli Asinelli (www.due-torribologna.com; daily Mar–Oct 9.30am–7.30pm, Nov–Feb 9.30am–5.45pm) and the **Torre Garisenda** (no access) are the most potent symbols of the medieval era, when Bologna bristled with around 120 towers. Both date back to the 12th century, and were probably built as watchtowers

Tilting towers

In 1786 the German writer Goethe, in unusually flippant mood, got the measure of the Bolognese nobility: "Building a tower became both a hobby and a point of honour. In time, perpendicular towers became commonplace, so everyone wanted a leaning one."

as well as status symbols. Legend has it that the two richest families in Bologna, the Asinelli and the Garisenda, competed to build the tallest and most beautiful tower in the city.

A sense of history and a bird's eye view over the terracotta rooftops should tempt you to the top of Torre degli Asinelli (over 97m/318ft). It is admittedly a steep climb, with a narrow spiral staircase of 498 steps, but worth the effort. From the top you can locate some of the other 20-odd surviving medieval towers and, weather permitting, the foothills of the Alps beyond Verona. Like most of Bologna's towers, the Due Torri are both tilting: Garisenda 3.33m (11ft) to the northeast, Asinelli 2.23m (7.3ft) to the west. Garisenda originally rose to 60m (197ft) but it was built on weak foundations, and for safety reasons 12m (39ft) was lopped off in the mid-14th century. From certain angles, however, the two towers appear to be the same height. Dante, who was briefly in Bologna during his exile from Florence, and saw the acutely tilting tower (before it was shortened), included it in *The Inferno*, where he compares it to the bending Antaeus, giant son of Poseidon, frozen in ice at the bottom of hell. His quote is engraved on a plaque at the base of the tower.

Palazzo della Mercanzia

Below the towers, but in no way inconspicuous, is the 17th-century church of **San Bartolomeo**, with a Renaissance portico. Look for the *Annunciation* by Francesco Albani in the fourth chapel of the south aisle, and the small *Madonna with Child* by Guido Reni in the north transept. On the north side of the square the intrusion of a starkly modern office building invariably caused a furore when constructed in the 1950s.

PIAZZA DELLA MERCANZIA

Heart of the commercial district since medieval times, **Piazza della Mercanzia** ❿ is dominated by the crenellated **Palazzo della Mercanzia**, formerly the merchants' exchange and customs house, now seat of Bologna's Chamber of Commerce. The Gothic facade is adorned by statues representing the city's patron saints who smile benignly on an economy once based on gold, textiles, silk and hemp, but now in thrall to local success stories such as silky La Perla lingerie, hemp-free Bruno Magli shoes and Mandarina Duck bags. The palace safeguards the original recipes of local specialities, such as Bolognese *tagliatelle al ragù* (with the real Bolognese sauce). Pappagallo (see page 109), a charming old-world institution in a beautiful 13th-century building on the piazza, is a good place to try it.

STRADA MAGGIORE

Running southeast from Piazza Mercanzia is **Strada Maggiore** or Main Street, with an almost uninterrupted succession of aristocratic residences. On the left-hand side, at No 26, is the **Casa Rossini ⓫**, the composer's home from 1829 and 1848. Just beyond it on the right is the lofty and quaintly porticoed **Casa Isolani**, one of the city's few surviving 13th-century houses. Beyond it the **Caffè Commercianti** (No 23c) is traditionally favoured by academic types including the late polymath and best-selling author, Umberto Eco. Modelled on a Parisian café, it has Art Deco and Art Nouveau touches, and makes a chic coffee or cocktail stop.

MUSEO INTERNAZIONALE E BIBLIOTECA DELLA MUSICA

A mere baton's throw from Rossini's home, the Palazzo Sanguinetti at No 34 Strada Maggiore is home to the delightful **Museo Internazionale e Biblioteca della Musica ⓬** (International

⊙ MOZART AND MARTINI

In Room 3 of the Museum of Music you can find memorabilia of the young Mozart including two versions of his entrance exam to the Accademia Filarmonica di Bologna. His written test did not comply with the strict academic rules, so Father Giambattista Martini, who had taught Mozart and recognised his genius, secretly handed him the correct version. The museum has two versions of his test below his portrait, one of which includes several mistakes. Mozart came to Bologna twice in 1770 when he was 14. On the first occasion he performed a private concert for Count Pallavicini in his palace in Via San Felice and stayed at the Albergo del Pellegrino, which no longer exists.

Museum and Library of Music; www.museibologna.it/musica; Tue–Sun 10am–6.30pm). Rossini and his second wife, Olimpia Pelissier, were hosted here by their tenor friend, Domenico Donzelli. The museum is a recognition of Bologna's musical status: nine rooms trace six centuries of European music through 80 rare and antique musical instruments along with scores, historical documents and portraits. Even those who are not fans of classical music will be entranced by the *trompe-l'œil* courtyard and the frescoed interiors, offering a rare chance to see how the Bolognese nobility lived. The salon-like atmosphere, reflected in the mythological friezes and whimsical pastoral scenes, makes this the most enchanting city palace. The music library, with over 100,000 volumes opened here in 2014, after its transfer from Piazza Rossini.

MUSEO CIVICO D'ARTE INDUSTRIALE E GALLERIA DAVIA BARGELLINI

Beside the Palazzo Sanguinetti looms the **Torre degli Oseletti**, a medieval tower which was originally 70m (230 ft) tall. At the junction of Strada Maggiore and Piazza Aldrovandi, you are unlikely to miss the 'Palace of the Giants', **Palazzo Davia Bargellini**, whose entrance is flanked by two Baroque telamones. The palace is home to the **Museo Civico d'Arte Industriale e Galleria Davia Bargellini** ⓭ (www.museibologna.it/arteantica; Tue–Fri 9am–1pm, Sat–Sun 10am–6.30pm; free), a collection of applied and decorative arts, and notably Bolognese paintings, many of which belonged the Bargellini family who started collecting in 1500. Works include Vitale da Bologna's famous *Madonna dei Denti* (Madonna of the Teeth), a *Pietà* (1368) by his contemporary Simone dei Crocifissi, and the *Giocatori di Dadi* (*The Dice Players*) by Giuseppe Maria Crespi (1740), who specialised in genre scenes with vivid chiaroscuro effects. The last room holds an 18th-century Bolognese puppet theatre.

Gothic Santa Maria dei Servi

SANTA MARIA DEI SERVI

Across the road is the lovely Gothic **Santa Maria dei Servi** ⓮ (Mon 7.30am–12.30pm, Tue–Sun 7.30am–12.30pm, 4–7pm; free), graced by an elegant portico. Work on the church started in 1346 but it was almost two centuries before completion. The most interesting works of art lie behind the elaborate altar including (on the right side) fragment frescoes on the ceiling by Vitale da Bologna and, in a chapel on the left which you have to light up, an *Enthroned Madonna* (1280–90) tradition-ally attributed to the great Tuscan master Cimabue, but now thought to be from his workshop.

SANTO STEFANO

From Strada Maggiore the **Corte Isolani** ⓯, entered under the portico of Casa Isolani, is a bijou warren that runs into Via Santo Stefano. Gentrification has turned this cluster of

Santo Stefano church complex

medieval palaces into chic art galleries, desirable apartments, wine bars and cafés. **Via Santo Stefano** is every bit as gracious as Strada Maggiore with late Gothic palaces once favoured by Bolognese silk merchants. Regular upward glances often reveal 12th-century tower-houses incorporated in late-medieval residences and embellished with Renaissance facades. **Piazza Santo Stefano**  is a gentrified neighbourhood square (though more triangular than square), at its most convivial during an antiques market or gourmet food fair. This sought-after quarter numbers the once-radical politician, Romano Prodi, among its ranks – proof, if needed, that politically red Bologna now prefers pale pink.

The cobbled piazza forms the intimate backdrop to **Santo Stefano** (daily 9.15am–7.15pm, winter until 6pm; free), the city's most hallowed spot. You will need plenty of time to appreciate and work out this ecclesiastical labyrinth, with its feast of ancient and medieval churches. Originally it was a complex of seven churches in one, as at Jerusalem, and it is known as Le Sette Chiese ('the Seven Churches') despite the fact that only four survive.

The complex dates back at least to the 5th century and may have been founded by Bishop Petronius as his cathedral on the site of a former pagan temple. His corpse was discovered here in

1141. The Lombards established their religious centre here, it then became a Benedictine sanctuary in the 10th century. Santo Stefano is still run by stern Benedictines who only soften when talking of the basilica's enduring appeal. One white-clad brother confides: "Dante often came here to meditate in 1287 but we are not fussy – at Easter even the local prostitutes come here for confession".

A harmonious ensemble is created by the interlocking churches and courtyards, including the Benedictine cloisters, graced by an elegant well head. Seen from the beautiful Piazza Santo Stefano the larger church on the right is the Chiesa del Crocifisso (Church of the Crucifix), the one in the middle the Church of San Sepolcro modelled on Jerusalem's Holy Sepulchre, and on the left Santi Vitale e Agricola, the oldest church in Bologna. Enter through the **Chiesa del Crocifisso**, of Lombard origin but which has undergone the most transformation. The church ends with a central stairway that climbs to the Presbytery. Steps lead down to a graceful little crypt, built to house the relics of the early Bolognese martyrs Vitale and Agricola who died around 304 AD. Their remains are contained in a golden urn on the altar. A door on the left of the main church leads into the most famous of the churches: the **Basilica of San Sepolcro**, a small and unusual polygonal, surrounded by columns, some of which survive from an ancient pagan temple. The body of St Petronius was found in this church in the mid-12th century; his relics used to lie in an urn in the centre of the small chapel but were transferred in 2000 to join the saint's head in the Basilica of San Petronio.

Bathed in mystical light the 11th-century **Santi Vitale e Agricola** is most compelling. Unadorned and built of bare brick it retains the most Romanesque Lombard character of all the churches in the city. It is dedicated to the first Bolognese martyrs, Vitale and Agricola, whose graves were discovered in 393 by the great bishop of Milan, St Ambrose. Adjoining it is the **Cortile di Pilato** (Pilate's Courtyard) a fine brick-walled courtyard with a large marble basin erroneously believed to have been used by Pontius Pilate to wash his hands. Under the arcades are chapels and tombstones. Beyond the courtyard lies the mystery **Martyrium**, a transverse church also named the Holy Cross or Trinity Church. Little is known of its origin and history. As you walk along there are niches that light up, one with a sculpted scene of the *Adoration of the Magi* by the Bolognese artist Simone de' Crocifissi. The courtyard leads into the peaceful Benedictine **cloister**, with two tiers of loggias. In the corner is a tiny museum of early Bolognese paintings and reliquaries, and a shop selling liqueurs and lotions made by Carmelite monks.

THE UNIVERSITY QUARTER

The University of Bologna, founded in the 11th century and famous in its early days for reviving the study of Roman law, is the oldest university in Europe. Petrarch attended classes here, as did Erasmus, Copernicus, various popes and cardinals – and more recently Guglielmo Marconi, Enzo Ferrari and Giorgio Armani. It is ranked the number one university in Italy and today attracts over 85,000 students annually from around the world. The heart of the student area is the triangle between Via Zamboni and Via San Vitale, but the university quarter also spills out onto Via delle Belli Arti. It is one of the most diverse districts, studded with churches, palaces and museums as well as arty bookshops, eclectic cafés, shabby-chic student dives and graffiti-splashed porticos. The curious Palazzo Poggi, sumptuous seat of the University, is home to several of the university's specialist museums and the Pinacoteca Nazionale boasts the richest art collection in the region.

The ornate Medicine faculty at the university

A leisurely stroll down Via Zamboni reveals the faculties of modern languages, philosophy, law, economics and the sciences, with each noble palace telling its own story. On the left, at No. 20, is the senatorial 16th-century **Palazzo Magnani** ⑱; its hall of honour is decorated with a stunning cycle of frescoes depicting the *The Story of the Foundation of Rome* (1592) by the three Carracci painters, Annibale, Agostino and Ludovico. The two brothers and their cousin worked collaboratively in their early careers and it is not easy to work out their individual contributions. The palace is the seat of UniCredit Bank but the frieze can be seen on request, at no charge – telephone one day in advance on 051-296 2508.

SAN GIACOMO MAGGIORE

Across the road lies **Piazza Rossini**, named after the composer who studied for three years (1806–9) at the Conservatorio G.B. Martini on the piazza. His first compositions and public performances date from this time, including a historic concert with the opera singer Isabella Colbran whom he married in 1822.

Overlooking the square is the church of **San Giacomo Maggiore** ⑲ (Mon–Fri 7.30am–12.30pm and 3.30–6.30pm, Sat–Sun 8.30am–12.30pm and 3.30–6.30pm; free), known as the Bentivoglio family's church. The Romanesque facade and portals flanked by lions pre-date Bologna's grandest dynasty but the elegant Renaissance portico dates from their era, as do many of the superb paintings in their family chapel (follow the sign as you enter the church). Although only open on Saturday morning (9.30am–12.30pm) the chapel can be seen through the railings and illuminated by inserting a 50 cent coin. The *Madonna and Child* (1488) and the eerie *Triumph of Death* and *Triumph of Fame* are all by the Ferrarese painter Lorenzo Costa who worked in Bologna before succeeding Mantegna as the principal painter at the Gonzaga court at Mantua. The *Madonna and Child* (the Bentivoglio Altarpiece) features Giovanni il Bentivoglio, his wife and eleven children and was allegedly commissioned in thanksgiving for the family's escape from an attempted massacre by a rival family. The *Madonna and Saints* (1494) by Francesco Raibolini, better known as 'Il Francia', is generally regarded as the best of the artist's many altarpieces.

ORATORIO DI SANTA CECILIA

Lorenzo Costa, Il Francia and contemporaries also worked on the **Oratorio di Santa Cecilia** ⑳ (daily Oct–May 10am–1pm and 2–6pm, June–Sept 10am–1pm and 3–7pm; free but donations welcome) which adjoins San Giacomo Maggiore and is accessed via the portico. This little gem was built in 1267 but remodelled by the Bentivoglios who commissioned the artists to portray the *Life and Martyrdom of St Cecilia*, patron saint of music. The lively but little known Renaissance fresco cycle starts with Cecilia's wedding (far left) and ends with her burial (far right). The scenes are accompanied by the bold statement 'the night after her marriage to a pagan youth, Cecilia revealed that she had taken a vow of chastity and persuaded her husband to convert as she was a bride of Christ'. Even so, the bride met a sticky end, boiled alive, then beheaded as portrayed in the gory decapi-

Teatro Comunale

tation scene on the left as you enter. St Cecilia is patron saint of music so it is appropriate that classical concerts (free of charge) are held in the oratory.

PIAZZA VERDI AND TEATRO COMUNALE

Further along Via Zamboni, **Piazza Verdi** ㉑ is a hub of student life. Café Scuderia, with tables spilling out onto the square, is all about chilling out over cheap coffee or beer. Music often wafts from the **Teatro Comunale** ㉒ (www.tcbo.it), the opera house overlooking the square. Originally called the Nuovo Teatro Pubblico, the theatre was built to replace the wooden Teatro Malvezzi destroyed by fire in 1745. In Renaissance times this was the site of the sumptuous, 244-room Palazzo Bentivoglio, which was sacked and destroyed in 1507 by the masses who had become discontented with the rule of the Bentivoglio dynasty. The adjoining Via Guasto (*guasto* meaning 'breakdown' or formerly

Museum of Human Anatomy exhibits inside the Palazzo Poggi

'devastation'), and the modern Giardini del Guasto derived their names from the ruins that laid here for decades. The 1930s facade of the Teatro Comunale belies an elegant Baroque-style interior with tiers of boxes (no access apart from performances). Many of these were formerly owned by titled families, each one individually decorated and bearing the family's coat of arms on the ceiling. The opera house played host to 20 operas by Rossini, who lived for many years in Bologna, as well as historic performances such as the premiere of Gluck's *Il Tronfio di Clelia* and the Italian premiere of Verdi's *Don Carlo* in 1867. It was also receptive to works of composers outside Italy and was the first Italian opera house to stage a Wagner opera, *Lohengrin*, in 1871. Today it is the city's main venue for opera (November to April), classical concerts and ballet.

PALAZZO POGGI

In 1803 the university moved from the Archiginnasio (see page 38) to the 16th-century **Palazzo Poggi** ㉓ (Via Zamboni 33; Tue–Fri 10am–4pm, Sat–Sun 10am–6pm; charge only for guided visits of the Specola, the Observatory, for which online reservations are required at http://museospecola.difa.unibo.it). This opulent seat of the university, decorated with Mannerist and early Baroque frescoes, is home to a confusing yet fascinating cluster of university museums. In the 17th and 18th centuries, this was the leading scientific institute in Europe, based on Bologna's history of scholarship, particularly in anatomy and astronomy. A visit to the **Specola** tower on a guided tour (in Italian and English) is highly recommended; it also includes the Specola Museum and its rich collection of instruments for astronomical studies such as medieval astrolabes and celestial and terrestrial globes. The tower was built on top of the building and served as an astronomical observatory.

The collections in the university served primarily for research rather than as attractions for visitors, but it's worth wandering through the vaulted frescoed galleries, with cycles of

---

⦿ MARCONI: BOLOGNA'S WIRELESS PIONEER

Among Bologna University's famous alumni is Guglielmo Marconi (1874–1937), known for his pioneering work on long-distance wireless communication. He was born in Bologna in 1874 to a wealthy Italian landowner and his Irish-Scots wife but when Italy showed no interest in his experiments or requests for funding he moved to the UK. At the age of 27 he succeeded in receiving the first transatlantic radio signal which led to a worldwide revolution in telecommunications. In 1909 Marconi shared the Nobel Prize in Physics for his work on wireless telegraphy. His Marconi Company radios saved hundreds of lives, including the 700 surviving passengers of the sinking *Titanic* in 1912. Bologna's airport was named after him in 1978. Some of Marconi's earliest experiments were completed at the family home, Villa Griffone at Pontechhio Marconi, 15km (9 miles) from Bologna, now home to the Marconi Museum (www.museomarconi.it; guided tours, reservation only).

16th-century frescoes, and picking out a few curiosities. Exhibits (many of which now have labels and explanations in English) range from models of military architecture and reconstructions of 17th-century warships to precious manuscripts and Japanese woodcuts. But the invariable magnets are the Museums of Obstetrics and Human Anatomy. Set up for teaching surgeons, doctors and midwives in the 18th century the collection includes a birthing chair on which students would practise blindfold as well as terracotta and wax models of wrongly-presented foetuses and gruesome models of human dissections.

There is more to see on Via Irnerio to the north of Palazzo Poggi: the university's Botanical Garden, Museum of Physics (currently closed) and the **L. Cattaneo Museo delle Cere Anatomiche** (Museum of Anatomic Wax Models; June–Aug

A painting depicting medieval Bologna at the Pinacoteca Nazionale

Mon–Fri 10am–1pm, Sat–Sun 10am–6pm, Sept–May Mon–Fri 9am–1pm, Sat–Sun 10am–6pm; free) at No 48, with more waxwork teaching aids, including models of faces with small pox and tumours, human intestines and conjoined twins.

> **Wise words**
>
> "When Bologna stops teaching, Bologna will be no more". The words of the Archdeacon of Bologna's cathedral and head chancellor of the Studium (University) in 1687.

PINACOTECA NAZIONALE

Just north of Palazzo Poggi, on Via delle Belle Arti is the **Pinacoteca Nazionale** ❷❹ (National Art Gallery; www.pinacotecabologna.beniculturali.it; Sept–June Tue–Sun 9am–7.30pm, July–Aug Tue–Wed 8.30am–2pm, Thu–Sun 1.45–7.30pm), the finest treasure house in the city. The National Gallery's only flaw is its tendency to close sections for 'lack of personnel'. Created during the Napoleonic occupation, the museum displays paintings plucked from demolished or deconsecrated churches. As was his wont Napoleon stole many of the finest treasures for the Louvre but Bologna managed to get them back in 1815. The gallery follows the path of Bolognese and Emilian art from the Middle Ages to the 18th century, but also includes works by artists from Florence, Tuscany and other 'foreign' parts, showing the influence on local artists.

The itinerary begins with works by Bolognese artists of the 14th century, and notably the vigorous and brilliantly coloured *St George and the Dragon* (c.1335) by Vitale da Bologna. Though cast in Byzantine-influenced Gothic mould, this dramatic, stylised scene shows the realism and expressiveness typical of Trecento Bolognese art. Other gallery scene-stealers are Giotto's luminous polyptych *Madonna and Child with Saints*, which takes pride of place in Room 3 as one of only three panel paintings in the world signed by the artist, and Raphael's *Santa Cecilia* (c.1515) in Room 15. This late altarpiece depicts the early Christian martyr and patron saint of music in ecstasy as she listens to a choir of angels in company of saints and Mary Magdalene. It was commissioned for a chapel dedicated to the saint in Bologna's Augustinian Church of San

⊙ BOLOGNA AND THE BAROQUE

The members of the Bolognese school exerted one of the main influences on Baroque painting in Italy in the 17th century. Agostino (1557–1602), Annibale (1560–1609) and Ludovico Carracci (1555–1619), two brothers and a cousin, were leading figures in the movement against the affectations of Mannerism in Italian painting. Much in keeping with the desires of the Counter Reformation they revived the tradition of solidity and grandeur of the High Renaissance, stressing rigorous draftsmanship from life. Annibale's fame was such that he was called to Rome to decorate the Farnese gallery, considered in its time as a worthy successor to the frescoes of Michelangelo and Raphael. Guido Reni (1775–1642) was a pupil of the Carracci and was initially influenced by their classicising style. He left Bologna for Rome where he painted many of his finest works, but returned to his native city in 1613 to head a vast studio that exported religious works all over Europe.

In the 19th century the Bolognese painters fell from favour. The leading art critic, John Ruskin, described the school as having "no single virtue, no colour, no drawing, no character, no history, no thought". Their status suffered from Ruskin's attacks but the Carraccis and Guido Reni are now regarded among the greatest Italian painters of their age.

Giovanni in Monte; from the same church came Parmigianino's *Madonna and Child with Saints* (c.1530) now opposite the Raphael.

Not to be missed are the works by the great Bolognese Baroque artists. Room 23 displays masterpieces by all three of the Carracci painters. The two brothers and their cousin worked collaboratively and their frescoes still adorn the greatest city palaces; but here the works by the individual artists highlight their differences in style as well as their similarities. Room 24 is dedicated to works by Guido Reni (1575–1642), including a portrait of his mother and the dramatic and skilful *Massacre of the Innocents*, distinguished by a bold use of colour and grace of line and form.

NORTH AND WEST OF CENTRE

From the maze of streets in the former Jewish ghetto to a cluster of medieval palaces and museums, this area of northern

Bologna is packed with cultural attractions. When you have had your fill of sightseeing, the main streets of Via dell'Independenza, Via Ugo Bassi and Via Rizzoli provide plenty of retail distraction.

THE JEWISH GHETTO

The cathedral's lofty interior

Tucked into the triangle of Via Oberdan, Via Zamboni and Via Valdonica, in the shadow of the Due Torri, the former **ghetto** ㉕ is about mood rather than monuments. As a liberal, cosmopolitan city Bologna welcomed Jews who were booksellers and drapers, but in 1555, under papal rule, the ghetto was established. Unlike the crisply geometric street plan in 'Roman' Bologna this area is a warren of narrow alleys, predating the papal edict. Take Via de Giudei (Street of the Jews) to moody Via Canonica and **Via dell'Inferno** ㉖. The appropriately named 'Hell Street' became a virtual prison as only doctors were allowed to leave the ghetto at night. A plaque records the Holocaust but makes no reference to the expulsion of the Jews from here in 1593. The lofty buildings in Via Valdonica reflect the fact that the ghetto could only expand upwards. Recent gentrification has turned these tall tenements into desirable designer pads, so Hell Street is now a prestigious address – and one with a growing number of artisan workshops such as Calzoleria Max & Gio at No 22A, creators of fine, made-to-measure shoes for men. The Palazzo Pannolini at 1/5 Via

Valdonica is home to the **Museo Ebraico** (Jewish Museum; www. museoebraicobo.it; Sun–Thu 10am–6pm, Fri 10am–4pm) which aims to preserve, study and promote the cultural Jewish heritage of Bologna and the Emilia Romagna region. The history of the Jewish population is analysed through multi-media exhibits, documents and artefacts from former ghettos.

North of the ghetto, on Piazza San Martino is **San Martino** (Mon–Sat 8am–noon and 4–7pm, Sun 8.30am–1pm and 4–7pm; free), a Carmelite church remodelled in the 14th century along Gothic lines. A quick visit reveals fragments of a Uccello battle scene and paintings by notable Bolognese artists, such as the Carracci. Also in this area look up to spot sealed arches and other vestiges of medieval churches, deconsecrated in Napoleon's day. But also expect signs for 'happy hour' and 'tattoos', proof that the university is nearby. Indeed, the square adjoins **Via Goito**, a popular place with students and a reminder that, for its size, Bologna has the greatest concentration of students in Italy.

CATTEDRALE METROPOLITANA DI SAN PIETRO

Via dell'Indipendenza was built to link the city centre and railway station in 1888. At its southern end the main landmark is the **Cattedrale Metropolitana di San Pietro** ㉗ (Mon–Sat 7.30am–6.45pm, Sun 8am–6.45pm; free). Despite its nominal cathedral status and monumental interior, San Pietro plays second fiddle to the basilica of the city's patron saint, San Petronio. Architecturally and artistically it is certainly no match. In 1582 Pope Gregory XIII promoted the Bishop of Bologna to Archbishop and hence the cathedral rose to the rank of 'metropolitan church'. It was remodelled to be a showpiece of papal power and apart from a few relics in the Crypt and the red marble lions from the original portal there is little trace of the original Romanesque-Gothic structure. Stroll down

Museo Civico Medievale

Via Altabella to see the soaring **bell-tower** which accommodates the *'la nonna'* (grandmother), the largest bell playable *'alla bolognese'*, a form of full circle ringing devised in the 16th century but which is sadly disappearing.

PALAZZO FAVA

Along **Via Manzoni**, west of Via dell'Indipendenza, the Fava palazzi are among the finest in the city. At No 2, the Palazzo Fava-Ghisilieri is now known simply as **Palazzo Fava** ❷ (www.genusbononiae. it; Tue–Sun 10am–7pm; access may be limited when exhibitions are not showing; combined ticket available for Palazzo Pepoli, Museo della Storia di Bologna and San Colombano and Tagliavini Collection). The palace was fully renovated as part of the Genus Bononiae project (see page 68) and reopened in 2011 as an exhibition centre. Blockbuster art shows are hosted here but it is also a treasure house of Carracci frescoes. In 1584 Filippo Fava commissioned Agostino, Annibale and Ludovico Carracci to decorate rooms on the *piano nobile* which gave rise to the first major fresco cycle of their career. This portrays the tragic tale of *Jason and Medea* and adorns the grand Sala di Giasone. Other halls of the palace were later decorated with scenes from Virgil's *Aeneid* by Ludovico and his pupils. On the ground floor of the palace two rooms display changing exhibits from the art collection of the Fondazione Cassa di Risparmio di Bologna.

MUSEO CIVICO MEDIEVALE

Next along is **Palazzo Ghisilardi Fava**, an archetypal Bolognese
Gothic palace now home to the **Museo Civico Medievale** ㉙
(Via Manzoni 4; www.museibologna.it/arteantica; Tue–Sun
10am–6.30pm), a non-fusty medieval museum whose superbly
arrayed medieval and Renaissance treasures illuminate the
cultural and intellectual life of the city. A graceful, galleried
courtyard leads to a series of elaborately sculpted sarcophagi depicting the greatest medieval scholars, and notably the
lecturers in law. The collection's highlights are the coffered

⊙ A SUBTERRANEAN SERENISSIMA

It might not look like Venice but Bologna has an intricate network of over 60km (37 miles) of waterways, most of them running underground. From medieval times water was the source
of economic progress and prosperity. The waters of the Save-
na, Reno and Aposa rivers were harnessed into canals both for
domestic use and to provide energy for trades, particularly for
the mills of the flourishing textile industry. Bologna became a
leading silk producer in the 15th century and at the height of
the industry had over 100 silk mills. The waterways were filled
in during the 19th century but a port on the Navile Canal took
goods and passengers down to the Po River and on to Venice, a system that served the city until the early 20th century.
For a glimpse back into the era of waterways head for the Via
Piella, just south of Piazza VIII Agosto, where the picturesque
view over the Reno Canal from the little 'window' on the bridge
gives a fleeting impression of Venice. For self-guided water-
way-themed tours visit www.bolognawelcome.com, and for
guided tours (in English and Italian) www.amicidelleacque.org.

Pick up a picnic

The covered Mercato delle Erbe at Via Ugo Bassi 25 (www.mercatodelleerbe.eu) is a great place for picnic supplies with its *salumerie* (for prosciutto and cheeses), bakers, *enotecas* and huge range of fresh fruit and veg. Alternatively there's a popular food court with a range of freshly prepared, affordable dishes.

ceilings, stone statuary, gilded wood sculptures, and the monumental crosses that once adorned major city crossroads. Among many remarkable works are the *Pietra della Pace*, Stone of Peace by Corrado Fogolini, 1322, in Room 9, celebrating peace between the university and municipality following a period of conflict; the red marble tombstone of Bartolomeo da Vernazza (1348) in Room 11 and the statue of a *Madonna and Child* in polychrome terracotta by Jacopo della Quercia (1410) in Room 12. More specialist are the bronzes, weaponry, miniatures, medals and musical instruments. The vast and bizarre bronze statue of Pope Boniface VIII (1301) by Manno da Siena in Room 7 is a reminder of how the papacy liked to exert its power. Beyond the museum, at No 6, is the Casa Fava Conoscenti, one of the rare surviving tower houses, dating back to the 13th century.

SAN COLOMBANO

Just to the west in Via Parigi the deconsecrated Church complex of **San Colombano** ❸ (www.genusbononiae.it; Tue–Sun 11am–7pm; combined ticket available for Palazzo Pepoli, Museo della Storia di Bologna and Palazzo Fava) makes a beautiful setting for the **Tagliavini Collection** of historical musical instruments. The late medieval church, decorated with faded frescoes, underwent major restoration before opening in 2010. Over 80 instruments are on display, among them spinets, harpsichords, clavichords and other keyboard instruments dating back five centuries and amassed by Bolognese musician and scholar, Luigi Ferdinando Tagliavini. Remarkably the instruments are all kept in perfect working order, played regularly and used for free monthly concerts from October to June. Among them are unique pieces such as an early 18th-century folding harpsichord and an earlier harpsichord with beautiful landscape decoration inside and out. The Oratory on the upper level displays a cycle of frescoes by the School of Carracci. Restoration works revealed the remains of a medieval crypt (accessible to the public) below the church, with a 13th-century mural *Crucifixion* attributed to Giunta Pisano and displayed behind glass.

Until Via dell'Indipendenza supplanted **Via Galliera** in 1888, this was the city's most majestic boulevard, built over a Roman road. The arcaded street is lined with noble palaces dating from the 15th to the 18th century. Here, as elsewhere, many of the terracotta-hued porticoes are built of recycled Roman and medieval bricks with decorative motifs in baked clay. The street runs north to the striking **Porta Galliera** (gateway), repeatedly destroyed and rebuilt five times between 1330 and 1511.

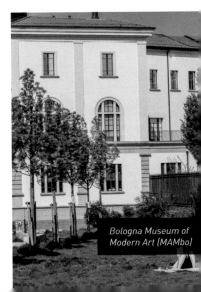

Bologna Museum of Modern Art (MAMbo)

The Fiera district

Northeast of centre the Bologna Exhibition Centre (www.bolognafiere.it) was built in 1961–75 beyond the ring road. It extends over 375,000 sq m (4,036,466 sq ft) and hosts around 30 exhibitions a year. During the most popular shows hotels in Bologna are booked up months in advance.

MAMBO

On the northwestern edge of the centre, transformed from a former municipal bakery which supplied bread to the Bolognesi during World War I, is **MAMbo** ❸❶ (Museo d'Arte Moderna di Bologna, Bologna Modern Art Museum; Via Don Minzoni 14; www.mambo-bologna. org; Tue, Wed and Fri–Sun 10am–6.30pm, Thu 10am–10pm). The museum forms part of the new cultural **Manifattura delle Arti** complex, transformed from the old harbour and industrial area of the city.

MAMbo hosts temporary exhibitions and has a permanent collection tracing the history of Italian art from World War II to the present day. It is also temporary home to the **Museo Morandi** – transferred from Palazzo d'Accursio in the centre while its galleries are undergoing restoration. Georgio Morandi (1890–1964) was one of the great still-life painters of modern times. This collection spans his Cézanne-influenced early works, his moody landscapes and his enigmatic bottles and bowls. Some of his less-opaque works are landscapes of the Bolognese hills, where the artist withdrew in the face of Fascism. Morandi fans can also now visit the recently restored house where Morandi lived and worked for most of his life, the **Casa Morandi** at 36 Via Fondazza, on the southeastern edge of the city (visits by appointment only, tel: 051-649 6611 or casamorandi@ comune.bologna.it).

SAN FRANCESCO

Feeling far removed from the city bustle, to the west of the centre is the Gothic **San Francesco** ㉜ (daily 6.45am–noon and 3.30–7pm; free). Despite radical restoration and serious damage during Allied bombardments in 1943, the Franciscan church remains one of the most beautiful in the city. Completed in 1263 it is now admired for its rebuilt Gothic facade, ornate altarpiece and Renaissance tombs, including, in the left aisle, the tomb of Pope Alexander V who died in Bologna in 1410. The precious marble altarpiece depicting saints and naturalistic scenes from the life of St Francis was the work of the Venetian artists, Pier Paolo and Jacobello dalle Masegne (1393). Outside, on the street side of the church, are the four raised **Tombs of the Glossatori** (legal annotators) dating from the 13th century. Before the university had a fixed abode students attended lectures in monastic churches, including this one, where medicine and arts were taught. The university's presence lived on in the tombs of these illustrious doctors of law and medicine.

SOUTH OF THE CENTRE

The cultural highlight of this quarter, south of the centre, is San Domenico, a convent complex and treasure house of art. The

Fiera district architecture

winding Via Castiglione at its northern end is lined by imposing mansions from various eras including the fortress-like medieval Palazzo Pepoli, recently reinvented as a modern history museum. Many of the terracotta-hued palazzi afford glimpses of vaulted courtyards, sculpted gateways and richly frescoed interiors. West of San Domenico Via Marsili and Via d'Azeglio form part of the city's *passeggiata*, or ritual stroll, a chance to see the city at its most sociable.

The Piazza della Mercanzia south of the Due Torri feeds into the noble end of **Via Castiglione**. Both this street and Via Farini, an elegant shopping street, conceal waterways. The canal network linked to the River Po and the Adriatic generated the power for the silk and paper mills, brickworks and tanneries and for the millers, dyers and weavers who were

⊘ GENUS BONONIAE, MUSEUMS IN THE CITY

The Museo della Storia di Bologna is one of the eight cultural attractions on the 'Genus Bononiae Museums in the City' itinerary (www.genusbononiae.it). The route takes in some of the city's most important churches and palaces that have been completely renovated for public use. Apart from one, all are within easy walking distance in the city centre. The attractions include the Palazzo Fava (see page 62) and the churches of San Colombano with the Tagliavini Collection (see page 64), Santa Maria della Vita (see page 41) and Santa Cristina, where concerts are held. Just out of town is San Michele in Bosco, a former monastery on a hill overlooking the city. The churches and palaces on the itinerary are managed, and some also owned by, the Fondazione Cassa di Risparmio di Bologna, a non-profit-making bank foundation.

the mainstay of the medieval economy. But when the district was gentrified in the 16th century, the nobility scorned these murky waters. Although finally covered in 1660, the canal still runs below Via Castiglione which explains why the pavements resemble canal banks.

The austere medieval facade of the **Palazzo Pepoli Vecchio** at No 8 Via Castiglione belies a brand new interior, home to the

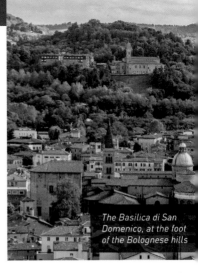

The Basilica di San Domenico, at the foot of the Bolognese hills

Museo della Storia di Bologna ❸ (Museum of the History of Bologna; www.genusbononiae.it; Tue–Sun 10am–7pm; combined ticket available for Palazzo Fava, Palazzo delle Esposizioni and San Colombano and Tagliavini Collection see pages 62 and 64). The grandiose palace was built as the seat of the Pepoli, lords of Bologna in the mid-14th century, but was not completed until 1723. The interior underwent a total transformation in 2012 to become an innovative, interactive museum, dedicated to the historical and cultural heritage of Bologna. The tour spans 2,500 years of the city's distinguished history, focusing around the futuristic steel and glass Torre del Tempo (Tower of Time) which rises up from the courtyard. Through 3D films (and cartoons), mock-ups of Etruscan and Roman roads, photos and multimedia installations, the museum traces the evolution of the city from the Etruscans to the present day. The lively modern displays tend to attract

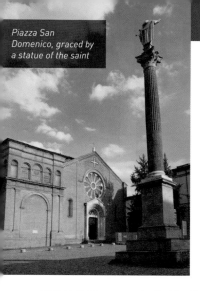
Piazza San Domenico, graced by a statue of the saint

more school groups and students than tourists and most of the labelling and videos are in Italian (though there are information sheets in English in most rooms).

BASILICA DI SAN DOMENICO

As you walk south along the Via Castiglione, the mood becomes subtly more domesticated. This was the key route to the Bolognese hills and access here was controlled by Porta Castiglione, one of ten surviving city gates. To the west the monumental **Basilica di San Domenico** ③④ (Mon–Fri 9am–noon and 3.30–6pm, Sat 9am–noon and 3.30–5pm, Sun 3.30–5pm; charge for presbytery only) dominates the cobbled **Piazza San Domenico**. The two mausoleums on the square, each with its tomb raised on pillars and protected by a canopy, celebrate renowned medieval law scholars Rolandino de' Passaggeri and Egidio Foscherari.

The Basilica was built to house the relics of San Domenico, founder of the Dominican order, who died here in 1221 when it was just the small church of San Nicolò of the Vineyards on the outskirts of Bologna. He was canonised in 1234 and his remains lie in an exquisite shrine within the church. The Dominican foundation was built in 1228–38 but was remodelled in Baroque style. Although it has lost much of its late Romanesque and Renaissance purity it abounds in curious, canopied tombs and artworks by such luminaries as Michelangleo, Pisano and Filippino Lippi as well as by leading Bolognese artists. The **Cappella di San Domenico** (Chapel of St Dominic) holding the saint's tomb is half way down the basilica on the right. The spectacular **Arca di San Domenico** (Tomb of St Dominic) is the work of various leading artists, among them Niccolò da Bari – who acquired the name Niccolò dell'Arca following his highly acclaimed work on this tomb – Niccolò Pisano and Arnolfo di Cambio, both of the Pisan School. Niccolò da Bari died in 1492 and the Arca was completed by Michelangelo (a mere 19 years-old at the time) who carved two Bolognese saints, St Proculus and St Petronius holding a model of Bologna, and the angel on the right of the altar table holding up the candelabra. Above the Arca, Guido Reni's *St Dominic in Glory with Christ, the Madonna and Saints* decorates the dome, and hidden behind the shrine lies the precious reliquary of the head of St Dominic. Among the many other art works are the *Crucifix* (1250) by Giunta Pisano and the tomb of Taddeo Pepoli both in the left transept, the *Mystical Marriage of St Catherine* by Filippino Lippi in the small chapel beyond the right transept and the beautiful mid-16th-century marquetry choir stalls.

VIA D'AZEGLIO

In the late afternoon and early evening the pedestrianised **Via d'Azeglio** ㉟, west

Bologna's beloved Lucio Dalla

If you happen to be in Via d'Azeglio at 6pm, you will hear the music of Lucio Dalla (1943–2012), the much-loved Bolognese singer-songwriter (his *Caruso* sung by Pavarotti sold nine million copies). The music is streamed from Via d'Azeglia 15, where Dalla lived. His funeral was held in the Basilica of San Petronio and over 50,000 people came to the Piazza to bid him farewell.

of San Domenico, is known as *il salotto*, or drawing room – the place for chatting over cocktails and designer shopping. It is a relaxed mix of happy families and glamorous Bologna *per bene* – the smart set. There are big-name boutiques here but the most sought-after shops are in neighbouring Galleria Cavour and Via Farini. The boldest of Bologna's senatorial palaces stands at No 31 – the 15th-century **Palazzo Bevilacqua** (No 31) in Tuscan style, with a rusticated sandstone facade, wrought iron balconies and a courtyard surrounded by a loggia. Here the Council of Trent met for two sessions in 1547 after fleeing an epidemic in Trent.

Tucked away in a corner west of Via d'Azeglio and off Via Collegio di Spagna lies a curious Spanish enclave. The crenellated **Collegio di Spagna** (visits only on request) was founded in 1365 by Cardinal Gil de Albornoz (representing the papacy) and bequeathed to Spanish scholars at Bologna University in 1365 as a glorified hostel. It continues to fulfil this function today, under the auspices of the Spanish Crown. Close by is the **Caffè de la Paix**, a café as peaceful as it sounds, with a special welcome for Spanish scholars. To the north east, on the corner of Via Val d'Aposa and Vicolo Spirito Santo, the **Spirito Santo** (no admission to the public) is an exquisite jewel-box of a church. Under the medieval streets here runs a secret river, the d'Aposa.

THE BOLOGNA HILLS

Crowning a hilltop to the southwest of the city and linked to it by the world's longest portico is the famous **Santuario della Madonna di San Luca** ③⑥ (Mar–Oct Mon–Sat 7am–12.30pm and 2.30–7pm, Sun 7am–7pm, Nov–Feb until 6pm; church: free, terrace: donation). Dating from 1732 the conspicuous pink basilica took 50 years to build, is 3.8km (2.3 miles) long, has 666 arches and winds its way up from Piazza di Porta

You'll never go hungry in Bologna

Saragozza. You are rewarded at the top with fine views of the Apennines. (If you don't fancy the whole hike take bus No 20 to the Arco Meloncello and walk from there or take the little tourist train from the centre in season.) The 18th-century sanctuary is richly decorated and houses a much-revered Byzantine-style image of the Madonna, probably dating from medieval times but once believed to have been painted by St Luke. Every Ascension Week she is taken down the hill to the Cathedral of San Pietro, with crowds lining the Via Saragozza to see the procession go by. The church brings barefoot pilgrims and other worshippers as well as joggers and cyclists who go up the hill to work off the pasta.

Lording it over Bologna to its south is **San Michele in Bosco** ③⑦ (daily 8am–noon and 4–6pm; free; 30 mins on foot or take No 30 bus), a religious complex with an annexed monastery that has served as an orthopaedic hospital since 1880. The Fondazione

Cassa di Risparmio di Bologna now manages the vast area, including the octagonal cloister and library, and the church complex features on the Genus Bononiae museum itinerary (see page 68). The sweeping views, which were admired by Stendhal when he passed through Bologna in 1817, embrace the entire city.

EXCURSIONS FROM BOLOGNA

With excellent rail links Bologna makes a good base for excursions to the handsome historic cities of Emilia-Romagna. (It is only around half an hour to Modena and Ferrara, an hour to Parma, 80 mins to Ravenna, 60–90 mins to Rimini). Apart from culture, the region is a gourmet's delight and many visitors come on gastronomic tours taking in artisan producers of Parma ham, Mortadella, traditional balsamic vinegar of Modena, Parmigiano Reggiano – as well as local wine producers. The Langhirano valley is home to around 500 authorised producers of the famous *prosciutto crudo* di Parma, many open to the public for tastings and purchases. On plains north of Parma there are Parmesan cheese-making cooperatives and around Modena balsamic vinegar distilleries where the vinegar is aged in wooden barrels for up to 25 years.

Frogs' legs fresco

A canon of Parma's cathedral criticised Correggio's fresco of the *Assumption of the Virgin* as 'a stew of frogs' legs', but Titian, recognising the artist's triumph of illusionism, decreed that if the dome were turned upside down and filled with gold it would not be as valuable as Correggio's frescoes.

PARMA

Parma ㊳ is a byword for fine living, from Parmesan and Parma ham to music and Mannerist art. At the heart of the city a network of quiet old streets opens on to the harmonious **Piazza Duomo** where the Lombard Romanesque **Cathedral** (www.piazzaduomoparma.com; daily 10am–6pm; church: free, baptistery: charge) and the graceful rose marble Baptistery form a fine ensemble. Inside the cathedral, decorating the central dome in a triumph of *trompe-l'œil*,

Al fresco dining in Parma

is Corregio's great masterpiece: the *Assumption of the Virgin (1526–30)*. This boldly illusionistic work, Corregio's last fresco, paved the way for Baroque art but found little favour with the church. The neighbouring **Baptistery** (daily 10am–6pm) is a jewel of the Italian Romanesque – a beautiful octagonal building with elaborately carved reliefs on the exterior and portals by sculptor and architect, Benedetto Antelami (1150–1230). The interior is an illuminated manuscript awash with vividly coloured 13th-century biblical scenes, influenced by Byzantine art. Antelami and his assistants created the series of sculptures, showing the seasons, the signs of the zodiac and the labours of the month. The masterly Antelami is also believed to have been the architect of the Baptistery.

Behind the cathedral the 16th-century Renaissance church of **San Giovanni Evangelista** (daily 8.30–11.45am and 3–6pm) with a Baroque facade also has a cupola decorated with a fine

Modena's Piazza Grande, dominated by the Romanesque Duomo

Correggio fresco: *The Vision of St John on Patmos*, depicting Christ descending to John. Northwest of Piazza del Duomo, in a former Benedictine convent, the **Camera di San Paolo** (Mon–Sat 1.10–6.50pm) was one of the private rooms in the apartments of the unconventional and learned Abbess of San Paolo, called Giovanna da Piacenza. In 1519 she commissioned Correggio to decorate the room with a feast for the senses, including mischievous *putti* and a view of Chastity as symbolised by the goddess Diana. It was Correggio's first large-scale commission in Parma.

The **Palazzo della Pilotta** on Piazzale della Pace is the city's cultural heart and home to the **Galleria Nazionale** (Tue–Sat 8.30am–7pm, Sun 1–7pm) with works by locals such as Correggio and Il Parmigianino, along with Venetian, Tuscan and other Emilian artists. The palazzo also houses the archaeological museum, housing pre-Roman and Roman artefacts, the Palatine Library and the **Teatro Farnese**, an imposing wooden theatre with a revolving stage, based on Palladio's masterpiece, the Teatro Olimpico at Vicenza. It is still used for theatrical performances.

MODENA

Modena ㊴ is the home of Pavarotti, Maserati and Ferrari, and its wonderfully preserved historic centre is Unesco-listed. Yet it is rarely visited by tourists. The success of the food, sleek Ferrari cars and ceramics industries has been instrumental in making tourism a mere after-thought in this cosseted land of plenty. A morning's sightseeing in the historic centre could be followed by a meal at an *osteria* ranking No 1 in the World's 50 Best Restaurants (in 2018) (see page 114 and reserve well in advance), then perhaps a visit to a traditional balsamic vinegar distillery, **Acetaia di Giorgio** (Via Cabassi 67; www.acetaiadi-giorgio.it) to learn the tricks of the trade and taste the unctuous Aceto Balsamico Tradizionale di Modena vinegar.

Modena's city centre is dominated by the **Duomo** (daily 7.30am–12.30pm and 3.30–7pm) one of the masterpieces of the Italian Romanesque for both its architecture and sculpture. The grandiose marble cathedral and adjoining bell tower are Unesco World Heritage Sites. In a tribute, rare for the 12th century, the names of both the architect, Lanfranco, and the master sculptor, Wiligelmo da Modena, are recorded on inscriptions on the facade. Countess Matilda of Tuscany, ruler of Modena, commissioned Lanfranco, the greatest architect of the time, to mastermind the cathedral which would house the remains of St Geminiano, patron saint of the city. Wiglielmo equalled him in creating the exuberant friezes of griffins and dragons, peacocks and trailing vine leaves. On the southern side, the main portal is flanked by stylised Roman-style lions; over the doorway on the left is Wiglielmo's finest work, the depiction of the *Creation and Fall of Adam and Eve*. On the northern side the sculptured Porta

Pavarotti's house

The House and Museum of Luciano Pavarotti, 8km (5 miles) from the centre of Modena (www.casamuseolucianopavarotti.it) gives a glimpse into the life of the late maestro. Opened in 2015, it displays personal memorabilia and recordings of great performances.

della Pescheria is decorated with the cycle of the months. The softly lit interior reveals brick-vaulted naves and such treasures as the rood-screen, a Romanesque masterpiece, as well as the crypt sculpted by Wiglielmo. Alongside the apse rises the leaning **Torre della Ghirlandina**, the octagonal 12th-century bell tower built with slabs of marble recycled from Roman ruins.

To the northwest of the cathedral, on Piazza Sant'Agostino, stands the **Palazzo dei Musei** (www.museicivici.modena.it) where the d'Este court amassed Modena's finest art collection and library and now hosting the city's museums and art galleries. The most interesting are the **Galleria Estense** (www.gallerie-estensi.beniculturali.it; Tue–Sat 8.30am–7.30pm, Sun 2–7.30pm), a rich collection of works by Emilian, Flemish and Venetian artists, and the **Biblioteca Estense** which displays rare manuscripts, seals and maps, as well as the priceless Bibbio Borso, the beautifully illustrated bible of Borso d'Este, first Duke of Modena. On Piazza Roma, northeast of the cathedral, the austere and immense **Palazzo Ducale** (Ducal Palace) was the former court of the d'Este dynasty. It is now Italy's top military academy, with no access for the public, but the ducal park behind has been converted into public and botanical gardens.

FERRARI MUSEUMS

Ferrari, Maserati and Lamborghini sports cars are all produced in Modena so a passion for speed goes with the territory.

Enzo Ferrari founded his firm in 1939 and the company is still producing cars in the Maranello factories in the industrial out-skirts. Modena now has its own Ferrari museum: the **Museo Enzo Ferrari** (https://musei.ferrari.com/en/modena) where Ferraris and Maseratis are displayed in a gigantic show-room and Enzo Ferrari's fascinating life story is related in the converted workshop of his father. A regular shuttle bus connects the museum with Maranello (20km/12.5 miles from Modena) where the **Museo Ferrari** (https://musei.ferrari.com/en/maranello) showcases the world's largest collection of Ferraris, with models through the ages – and a simulator where visitors can experience driving a Ferrari single-seater on the Monza track. Every Ferrari victory in the Grand Prix is celebrated by the priest ringing the bells of the Maranello parish church – which gives you some idea of the fanaticism of the locals.

FERRARA

Beguiling **Ferrara** ⓵ was a stronghold of the high-living dukes of Este – archetypically schem-ing, murderous, lovable Renaissance villains who ruled from 1200–1600 and from Ferrara-controlled territory embracing Parma, Modena and Garfagnana in Tuscany. During its Renaissance heyday, the dynasty drew artists of

The gleaming Museum Enzo Ferrari in Modena

On your bike

Ferrara is Italy's most bike-friendly city – there are 2.1 bikes per inhabitant. For bike-hire, cycling suggestions in the traffic-free centre and cycling tourism in the province (including the popular 100km/62.5 mile route that runs along the River Po towards the sea) visit www.ferrateraeacqua.it.

the stature of Piero della Francesca and Mantegna, turning the Ferrara court into a 'princely garden of delights'. From the 17th to the 19th century travellers found Ferrara something of a ghost town with few inhabitants and grass growing in the streets. However since its bombing in World War II the city has revived and in 1995 was declared a Unesco World Heritage Site.

The heart of the town is still dominated by the formidable **Castello Estense** (www.castelloestense.it; Oct–Feb Tue–Sun 9.30am–5.30pm, Mar–Sept daily 9.30am–5.30pm), a 14th-century moated fortress where guides tell delightfully dubious tales of what went on in the dungeons. As the d'Este dynasty's seat the medieval fortress was gradually transformed into a gracious Renaissance palace but retains elements from both incarnations. Most of the artistic treasures were spirited away to Modena when Ferrara's rival became the Ducal capital in 1598, and the great works of the Ferrarese school are dispersed in European public collections, notably the National Gallery in London. However the noble apartments retain some outstanding frescoed ceilings. To sample noble dishes dating back to the d'Este court, head for the **Hostaria Savonarola** in Piazza Savonarola, adjoining Castle Square. Try a plate of *tortelli di ricotta* or *cappellaci di zucca,* pumpkin-filled pasta parcels.

South of the Castello Estense is the triple-gabled Romanesque and Gothic **Cathedral** (Mon–Fri 7.30–11am and

4–7pm, Sat 7.30am–noon and 3–7pm, Sun 7.30am–1pm and 3.30–8pm; free). The facade has rich sculptural detail: from the lunette of *St George Killing the Dragon* to the loggia and the baldachin adorned with sculptures of the Madonna and Child. The disappointing Baroque interior is redeemed by a Byzantine baptismal font and the museum, which holds sculptures by Jacopo della Quercia and two masterpieces by Cosmè Tura decorating organ shutters and representing *The Annunciation* and *St George and the Princess*. The **Piazza della Cattedrale** is best appreciated from the café terrace of the Pasticceria Leon d'Oro. The piazza comes alive during the Palio in May, a medieval tournament dating back to 1259, and the Buskers' Festival in August, which is the biggest of its kind in the world.

Almost every vermillion brick palazzo in Ferrara has a link to the powerful dynasty. You can get a sense of their grandeur among the Renaissance palazzi of the Corso Ercole I d'Este, part of an ambitious 15th-century urban expansion, Addizione Erculea. The d'Estes' **Palazzo dei Diamanti** (www.palazzodiamanti. it; daily 9am–7pm) takes its name from the 8,500 diamond-shaped marble stones on its facade. The palace stages prestigious modern-art exhibitions and is also home to the

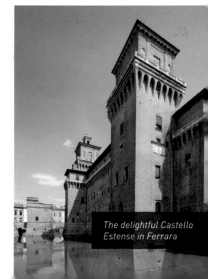
The delightful Castello Estense in Ferrara

Ravenna, one-time capital of the Western World

Pinacoteca Nazionale (www.gallerie-estensi.beniculturali.it; Tue–Sun 10am–5.30pm), which displays frescoes from several ruined churches and School of Ferrara paintings by Cosmè Tura and Francesco del Cossa.

The main thoroughfare, **Corso Giovecca**, has a sweep of patrician palaces designed to link the medieval core with the Renaissance city. The most regal residence is **Palazzina di Marfisa d'Este** (Tue–Sun 9.30am–1pm and 3–6pm) which was a *delizia*, a Renaissance pleasure palace dedicated to satisfying every whim. The noble apartments feature Renaissance furniture, a portrait gallery and ceilings studded with grotesque motifs. The frescoed loggia, which is used for concerts, is a lingering terrace of the sumptuous rural retreat that this once was.

On the south-eastern edge of the city the 14th-century **Palazzo Schifanoia** (closed for restoration at the time of writing) was the summer residence of Borso d'Este, Duke of Ferrara. The name translates as 'Palace for Banishing Boredom', a reflection of its role as the d'Este court's first and finest pleasure palace. The austere facade was once as richly frescoed as the interior. A highlight of the palace-museum is the restored **Salone dei Mesi** (Room of the Months) on the first floor which is decorated with a delightful cycle of frescoes depicting the four seasons. Here allegorical tales are interwoven with everyday scenes of the court.

RAVENNA

With its air of quiet prosperity, **Ravenna** ❹ seems like a provincial sleepy town that just happens to contain the finest mosaics in Europe. It has no less than eight Unesco World Heritage Sites in the shape of Byzantine mosaics. Like Venice, Ravenna was built on a series of islands in a lagoon. It thrived as a Roman city, was the last enclave of the Roman Empire in the West and even shone throughout the so-called Dark Ages. In the 5th and 6th centuries, Roman and Byzantine cultures converged in Ravenna and bequeathed the city superb mosaics, transforming it into a luminous Western Byzantium. Since the early mosaics were designed by Greek artists from Constantinople, the inspiration was as much from pagan temples as Christian churches.

In the northern corner of the city centre is the three-storey brick **Basilica of San Vitale** (daily Mar–Oct 9am–7pm, Nov–Feb 9am–5pm; ticket includes entry to Basilica of Sant'Apollinare Nuovo, Neoniano Baptistery, Mausoleum of Galla Placidia and Archiepiscopal Museum and Chapel and the opening times are the same). This simple octagonal-plan brick church, consecrated in the 6th century, has an interior decorated with superb mosaics, remarkable for their clarity of design and colour and their intricate detail. In the same grounds is the oldest of the Byzantine monuments, the 5th-century **Mausoleum of Galla Placidia**, named after the Christian half-sister of Honorius, the Roman emperor who transferred the capital to Ravenna in AD 402. She ruled in the emperor's absence, and later married a Visigoth king and a Roman emperor before returning to Ravenna. This tiny Latin cross-shaped mausoleum has a plain

brick exterior but inside a stunning tapestry of mosaics – the oldest in Ravenna. The mystical atmosphere is intensified by the strikingly simple style of the mosaics, including the cobalt-blue sky sprinkled with gold stars.

East of the city centre, the **Basilica di Sant'Apollinare Nuovo** was built by the Christian Ostrogoth King Theodoric in the 6th century using Greek marbled columns recycled from a pagan temple. The mosaic-encrusted interior is studded with scenes recalling life in Ravenna and biblical anecdotes. On the left, the mosaics depict 22 virgins leaving the ancient port of Classe to follow the Three Magi; opposite the solemn procession of 26 martyrs is wonderfully naturalistic, despite a traditional format. Although created in different periods the mosaics present great unity, infusing Byzantine decorative genius with the awe and mystery of Catholicism. These elements come together in a sublime *Christ in Majesty*.

Some 5km (3 miles) south of the centre stands the Byzantine **Basilica di Sant'Apollinare in Classe** (Mon–Sat 8.30am–7.30pm, Sun 1–7.30pm). If this sumptuous basilica seems marooned in the countryside, it is symbolic of the abandonment of the site after the silting up of Classe, Rome's largest Adriatic port. The focus of attention is the apse and choir with breathtaking mosaics, full of lovely landscape details. The presence of the docile lambs in the pastoral scene of the Good Shepherd leading his flock is a reminder that Ravenna was a beacon of artistic excellence at a time when sheep were grazing on the Roman forum. The lustrous tints and textures led Dante, who had sought refuge in Ravenna, to describe the mosaics as having 'the sweet colour of oriental sapphires'.

RIMINI

A long sandy beach, lively hotels and nightclubs make **Rimini** ⓸ a favourite playground for sun-seekers. But inland, on the other side of the railway, it has a quiet historic centre which retains Roman and Renaissance monuments. The most prized monument is the unfinished 15th-century **Tempio Malatestiano** (Mon–Fri 8.30am–noon and 3.30–6.30pm, Sat 8.30am–12.30pm and 3.30–7pm, Sun 9am–12.30pm and 3.30–6.30pm; free), a Renaissance design of the famous Florentine architect and art theorist Leon Battista Alberti, who was inspired by the wealth of Roman architecture remaining in the city. More pagan temple than church, it served as a mausoleum for the cultivated but cruel tyrant Sigismondo Malatesta and his wife Isotta degli Atti. Now the city cathedral, the Tempio showcases a crucifix attributed to Giotto, as well as Piero della Francesca's fresco of *Sigismondo Malatesta Kneeling before his Patron Saint Sigismondo* (1451) and the sculpted Malatesta tombs – works far finer than the debauched rulers deserved.

Designer shops line the elegant
Portico del Pavaglione

WHAT TO DO

ENTERTAINMENT

Bologna is lively all year round, but particularly from March to June and September to December when the cultural season is in full swing. The huge student population ensures that the city has a vibrant nightlife scene – during term-time at least; and during the long summer holiday, when the students abandon the city, the authorities stage a season of music and cinema to content its visitors. Bologna stages great music, both classical and contemporary, and is the only Italian city to have been appointed a Unesco Creative City of Music (2006). The tourist office website (www.bolognawelcome.com) is a good source of information for the host of cultural events and the venues for nightlife.

CLASSICAL MUSIC, OPERA AND THEATRE

The **Teatro Comunale** (Largo Respighi 1; www.tcbo.it) is the main venue for the performing arts, from opera and ballet to orchestral and chamber music. Tickets are available from the box office, the Bologna Welcome tourist office in Piazza Maggiore or online. Concerts are also organised in other city theatres, churches and at the **Conservatorio G.B. Martini** (Piazza Rossini 2; www.consbo.it), a concert hall within a former Augustine convent. Many churches, such as Santo Stefano, San Domenico, Santa Maria dei Servi and Santa Cristina, double up as concert venues. The frescoed **Museo Internazionale e Biblioteca della Musica** (Strada Maggiore 34, www.museibologna.it) is both an exceptional museum of music and a venue for classical concerts and events; likewise the restored church of **San Colombano** is home to the Tagliavini collection of

Sotto le stelle del Cinema
al 20 giugno al 30 luglio piazza Maggiore

Sotto le stelle del Cinema, a popular open-air film festival held in Piazza Maggiore in July

historical musical instruments and hosts free monthly classical concerts from October to June. The central **Auditorium Teatro Manzoni** (Via De'Monari ½; www.auditoriumanzoni.it), set within a finely restored Art Nouveau palazzo, hosts a range of concerts from classical to jazz, rock and contemporary. The **Teatro Europa** (Piazza Costituzione 4; www.teatroeuropa.it) is a multi-purpose venue for ballet, musicals and drama located near the Fiera exhibition centre.

CINEMA

The **Cineteca di Bologna** (www.cinetecadibologna.it) is located within the transformed Manifattura Tabacchi, a former tobacco factory on the northwest edge of the city, and now a major cultural centre. The Cineteca's state-of-the-art Cinéma Lumière (with the Sala Scorsese and Sala Mastroianni) honours the history of the moving image, screening restored classics, retrospectives and rare films always in the original version. The Cineteca also hosts Bologna's film festivals. Within the same complex is the Renzo Renzi Library, dedicated to the conservation and study of film and photography and the archives of Charlie Chaplin and Pier Paolo Pasolini (viewing by appointment only). The **Capitol** cinema (www.capitolmultisala.com) near the station shows blockbusters in their original version, with Italian subtitles.

NIGHTLIFE

As a lively university city, Bologna has no shortage of bars, pubs, clubs, live jazz and late-opening restaurants. The early evening involves the ritual *passeggiata*, the people-watching parade, partly viewed from a succession of café terraces. In summer Bologna's parks are transformed into party venues, with the atmosphere resembling a less boisterous version of a German *Biergarten*. The most popular spot is **La Montagnola Park** which has live jazz and rock music, as well as stalls selling beer, wine and fast food. Open-air concerts, films and festivities are also staged in city squares, such as Piazza Maggiore; other events take place in streets, museums and under the porticoes.

In general the liveliest area in town is the **Via Zamboni** in the university district which has the greatest concentration of late-night music haunts. The **Via del Pratello** area on the west side of the city also appeals to night-owls with pubs and bars (frequently serving food as well as drinks) interspersed with music clubs and inns. The nightlife is predominantly student-orientated although there are bar-restaurants that appeal to all ages. A good example is **Cantina Bentivoglio** (www.cantinabentivoglio.it) where the best jazz in Bologna can be enjoyed in palatial 16th-century cellars. An equally ageless, classless place is **Osteria de' Poeti** (www.osteriadepoeti.com) where, along with a friendly owner, brick-vaulted ceilings, 16th-century stonework and picturesque wine barrels provide a mellow mood for live jazz and folk music. Jazz has been thriving since the arrival of American troops at the end of World War II and can be heard in many other *osterie* throughout the city.

SHOPPING

Bologna's best buys are food and wine, fashion and designer goods. Shopping here is anything but provincial, and ranges from one-off boutiques to top designer brands – many of which started out in the city or in the wider region. Bologna's up-market fashion outlets are all central, and clustered around the Piazza Maggiore area, some in beautifully restored palazzi. The pedestrianised Via d'Azeglio is a lovely place to shop, as is Via dell'Archiginnasio, the porticoed area behind San Petronio known as the Pavaglione. The smartest boutiques line Via Farini and the discreet shopping galleries nearby. Galleria Cavour, a luxurious arcade linking Via Farini with Via de'Foscherari, is the place to go for the big designer brands. More mainstream shopping, from high fashion to footwear, can be found along Via dell'Indipendenza, Via Rizzoli and Via Ugo Bassi, the high streets of Bologna. Coin, at Via Rizzoli 7, part of the chain department store, is worth checking out for affordable clothes made in Italy.

⊙ APERITIVO TIME

Cocktails are part of Bolognese nightlife and Happy Hour is a moveable feast, from 6–9.30pm. The price of a drink may seem steep, but *stuzzichini* (appetizers) and often a whole buffet may be included and can provide a meal in itself. A favourite cocktail is an Aperol Spritz, made with orange liqueur, prosecco and a splash of soda. Among the popular cocktail spots are: Zanarini behind the Basilica, rendez-vous of well-heeled Bolognesi; Eataly, the popular 'marketplace' Italian chain at Via degli Orefici; and Ex Forno, the trendy café at the Bologna Museum of Modern Art. But the most unusual spot has to be the atmospheric Le Stanze (see page 112) housed within a Bentivoglio chapel.

GASTRONOMY

Bologna has a dazzling array of gastronomic delicacies. Moreover, Emilia Romagna, as a region, is dedicated to preserving its unique branded produce, from Parmesan cheese and Parma ham to balsamic vinegar, extra-virgin olive oil and wine. All of these can be picked up in delicatessens, markets, or sampled directly from the producers. The Bolognesi attach great importance to

Giorgio Armani was born in nearby Piacenza

finding the right foodstuffs and you are likely to find good quality just about everywhere, even in the simplest street market.

The Bologna Welcome office (www.bolognawelcome.com) has information on gastronomic tours where you can track down tasty cheeses, cured meats, truffles, dried mushrooms and genuine balsamic vinegar – just to name a few. In central Bologna, just off Piazza Maggiore, the warren of alleys making up the **Mercato di Mezzo** is a feast for the eyes with its specialised food shops, stalls piled high with fresh fruit, fish and cheese and a covered market which sells the finest regional produce. Along Via Pescherie Vecchie, Via degli Orefici and Via Drapperie shopkeepers tempt passers-by with slices of *mortadella* and *prosciutto*. **Tamburini** (Via Caprarie 1; www.tamburini.com) is the city's most endearing delicatessen, brimming with Bolognese and Emilian specialities. Try them out at their VeloCibò self-service. For homemade pasta and bread look no further than **Paolo Atti &**

Food shopping is
an art in Bologna

Figli (Via Caprarie 7; www.
paoloatti.com), a Bolognese
institution dating back to
1900 and still in the same
family. Pastas are all made
on the spot and their beautifully wrapped and boxed
creations make perfect
Italian gifts to take back
home. Also in the heart of
the market is **Salumeria
Simoni** (Via Drapperie 5/2a;
www.salumeriasimoni.it)
which is stacked to the brim
with hams and cheeses. A
step inside the shop may
well tempt you to sign up for one of their gastronomy tours or at
least to try out the delicacies with local wine.

Chocoholics should head for **Majani** (Via Carbonesi 5; www.
majani.it), one of Italy's oldest chocolate shops whose delicacies were one-time favourites with European royalty. Displays
are laid out in a splendid Art-Nouveau shop-front and Art-Deco
interior. Try the Fiat Majani, created for the launch of the new
Fiat Tipo 4, hence the four layers of velvety chocolate. Another
irresistible *chocolatier* is **Roccati** (Via Clavature 17a; www.
roccaticioccolato.com) where you can watch the chocolate
creations being sculpted in the workshop. Their speciality is
gianduja, chocolate with hazelnut. For divine patisserie head
for **Regina di Quadri** on Via Castiglione (www.pasticceriaregi
nadiquadri.it), with its show-stopping cakes and pastries.

Modena is renowned for *aceto balsamico* (balsamic vinegar)
but the factory-produced variety made of wine vinegar bears

scant resemblance to the traditional product – a subtle, unctuous substance that can only be sold after ageing in wooden casks for at least 12 years (red label), 18 years (silver label) or 25 years (gold label). Look for *Aceto Balsamico Tradizionale di Modena* or *di Reggio Emilia*. The real thing is a reduction of pressed and cooked Trebbiano and Lambrusco grapes, with a complex sweet and sour flavour, a hint of wood, and a high price tag. Expect to pay €40–80 for a small bottle, but whether you are using it on Parmigiano Reggiano and *mortadella* or drizzling it over strawberries or *gelato*, all you will need is a few drops. Bottles can be bought from *acetaie* (balsamic

◉ PASTA PERFECT

What better souvenir than to be able to recreate perfect hand-made pasta back home? Bologna has over 20 cookery schools, which is perhaps not surprising in what is generally regarded as the culinary capital of Italy. A half-day course might take in a tour of the local market with its fresh produce and gourmet delis (with tastings on the way) and a lesson on how to make an authentic *ragù alla bolognese* (bolognese sauce) and prepare the egg pasta from scratch. After all the hard work you can sit back and enjoy the fruits of your labour – along with a glass or two of good vino. The hands-on lessons are adapted to level of experience and culinary requirements; they are usually held in very small groups and last a couple of hours, a half or whole day or longer. A few days' notice may be required, though last-minute requests are always worth trying. Costs vary considerably from €90–160 for a half-day class (followed by lunch, which is included in the price). Full details are available from the Bologna Welcome tourist office (www.bolognawelcome.com).

Markets and food stalls abound with locally grown fruit and vegetables

vinegar producers) in the region or from high-end food shops in Bologna.

There are several excellent *enoteche* (specialised wine stores) where you can try and buy local wines, among them **Enoteca Italiana** (Via Marsala 2b) with a wonderful selection of Italian and particularly Emilia Romagna wines. It is run by two award-winning sommeliers who will guide you round – and suggest wines to go with regional treats such as Parma ham and *mortadella* which are served here all day.

MARKETS

The city markets are full of character, atmosphere and delicious foodstuffs, ideal for picnics or as presents to take home. In the centre are the **Mercato di Mezzo** and adjoining open-air food market as well as the renovated **Mercato delle Erbe** at Via Ugo Bassi 25, a large and lively covered market with wonderful local produce and a new food court where you can sit and make the most of prepared market produce. The **Mercato Antiquario**, occupying Piazza Santo Stefano and the streets nearby, is an antiques and curios market, with vintage clothing and jewellery, held on the second Saturday and Sunday of the month from 8.30am–6pm (7pm in summer, closed July and Aug). Another antiquarian fixture is the **Mercato dell'Antiquariato** on Via

Matteotti on the first Tuesday of the month (except for July and Aug) and from Mar–June and Sept–Dec also the third Tuesday of the month. The **DecoMela Art** and **San Giuseppe Colours** on Via San Giuseppe, which take place on alternative weekends (Fri–Sun except Jan, July and Aug), are handicraft-collectors' haunts, with pottery, lamps, fabrics and semi-precious stones. **La Piazzola** market occupies the Piazza VIII Agosto every Friday and Saturday and is worth checking out for bargain shoes and clothes, including vintage; it also sells leather, bric-à-brac, arts and crafts.

SPORT

Basketball (*pallacanestro*) in Bologna is hugely popular and the city's Virtus team (www.virtus.it) is one of the best in Europe. Tickets are available at www.ticketone.it or at the Unipol Arena in Casalecchio di Reno, southwest of the city, where they play. Their home rivals are Fortitudo (in the 2nd Division) who play at PalaDozza (or 'the Palazzo'), a multipurpose arena with a capacity of 5,570 in Piazza Azzarita, northwest of the centre. As elsewhere in Italy **football** (soccer) is a passion. Bologna FC (Football Club, www.bolognafc.it) in the First Division has won the Italian league championship seven times, and when they are playing at home thousands of fans will be heading to the Renato dall'Ara stadium, Via Andrea Costa 174, about 3km (2 miles) west of the city centre. Tickets can be bought at various tobacconists or online at https://sport.ticketone.it.

MOTOR VALLEY

In the heart of Emilia's 'Land of Motors', with its Ferrari and Lamborghini-inspired museums, Bologna is a motor-lover's dream. The museums can be visited independently by public transport or on a guided tour – details of which can be found at the Bologna Welcome tourist office and on their website (www.bolognawelcome.com). For the Ferrari Museums in Maranello and Modena see page 78. The **Museo Ferruccio Lamborghini** (www.museolamborghini.com) moved in 2013 from Dosso near Ferrara to Argelato, 15km (9 miles) north of Bologna. Visitors who book ahead can tour the company factory with Fabio Lamborghini, a nephew of the famous founder Ferruccio. For motorbike fans the **Ducati Museum** at the Ducati Factory (www.ducati.com/ww/en/ducati-museum-and-factory/museum), 9km (5.5 miles) northwest of the city centre, displays the models that have made the brand famous worldwide.

ACTIVE PURSUITS

Few of the central hotels have fitness centres but to get rid of excess tortellini you could climb the Asinelli Tower (498 steps), stretch your legs in the Parco della Montagnola or Giardini Margherita or walk 6km (4 miles) up to the hilltop sanctuary of San Luca.

The city is well equipped with public swimming pools including the **Piscina Sterlino** (Via A. Murri 113) southeast of the city, with one Olympic-sized pool, two 25m ones and a green area with bar, parasols and sunbeds in summer, and the **Carmen Longo-Stadio** at Bologna's football stadium centre (Via dello Sport, www.sogese.com), with indoor and outdoor pools. The **Circolo Tennis Bologna** (Viale Rino Cristiani 2; www.circolotennisbologna.com) in the Margherita Gardens has seven courts, floodlit from April to September and covered for the rest of the year. It also has a 25m swimming pool and a gym. For relaxation and wellbeing, the **Mare Terme San Petronio** (Via Irnerio 12/A; www.maretermalebolognese.it), near Parco della Montagnola, offers thermal spa waters, sauna, pool, hot tubs and beauty treatments. For those who prefer a Turkish bath the **Hammam**

Fabulous cars at the Museo Ferruccio Lamborghini

Bleu (Vicolo Barbazzi 4; www.hammam.it), centrally located just south of the Basilica of San Petronio, has treatments ranging from basic (€55) to the full works (€185). Booking is essential, as is a membership fee of €10 per person.

SPORTS IN EMILIA ROMAGNA

Emilia Romagna can compete with the sportiest of regions, with activities ranging from sailing to cycling, riding to alpine skiing, ice-skating to Formula One racing. The landscape lends itself to a wealth of possibilities: the lofty Apennines become small-scale ski slopes in winter but revert to rugged open-walking country in spring and summer. The flat area around Ferrara is gentle cycling country with inviting tracks created on the raised canal banks in the Po Delta area. The Ferrara tourist authorities have set up superb cycling routes, with guides, to get you effortlessly around the Po Delta. The region is well endowed with 'bike hotels' – places offering a full service from picnic hampers to bike repairs and maps for the next stretch of route.

CHILDREN'S BOLOGNA

Bologna is not the obvious choice for children, especially given the sparsity of parks and gardens in the centre. Active youngsters might enjoy the challenge of 498 steps up the **Torre degli Asinelli**, older ones will no doubt be fascinated by the **Teatro Anatomico** where human dissections took place, the **Specola** (Observatory) and **waxwork museums** of the University (see page 55). The innovative **Museum of History at Palazzo Pepoli** is geared to all ages with 3-D films and reconstructions, and the **Sala Borsa multimedia centre**, right in the centre, is a good place to chill out

Ice cream is always a winner

with computers or watching films. Take sports fans to see Virtus play **basketball** and to let off steam **climb** (or jog/bike up) the world's longest portico to the Sanctuary of the Madonna di San Luca. The best park for picnics (or snacks at the Chalet dei Giardini Margherita on the bridge over the central lake) is the **Giardini di Margherita**, just beyond the southern city walls. In the **Parco della Montagnola**, children can enjoy a variety of shows and themed activities.

CALENDAR OF EVENTS

Arte Fiera Last weekend of January. Dedicated to contemporary art, with exhibitions and events throughout the city.

Children's Carnival. February. Allegorical floats and parades in the city centre

Children's Book Fair. Early April. The most important of its kind in the world.

Live Arts Week. 3rd week April. Festival of contemporary performing arts.

Madonna di San Luca Ascension Day. Heartfelt festival in honour of the icon of the Virgin in San Luca, with a procession through the city.

Future Film Festival Late May. International festival of cinema, animation and new technologies.

Diverdeinverde 3 days, late May. Private gardens in Bologna and surrounding hills open to the public.

Bè Bolognaestate June-September. Summer programme of music, art and theatre throughout the city.

Il Cinema Ritrovato Late June/early July. Celebration of film classics with screenings, including rare movies, in various cinemas and on Piazza Maggiore.

Danzaurbana September. International festival of contemporary dance.

Bologna, La Strada del Jazz Mid-September. Jazz concerts and events in the Quadrilatero.

Festa di San Petronio 4 October. Feast of the patron saint with concerts and other events taking place from 1st–4th October.

Bologna Jazz Festival October–November. Almost a month of concerts with well-known Italian and international jazz artists.

Gender Bender Late October/early November. International interdisciplinary festival dedicated to gender identity and sexual orientation.

Trekking Urbano Bologna Last weekend October. Guided tours to discover Bologna and surroundings.

Cioccoshow November. Four- or five-day event dedicated to top-quality chocolate, with tastings, stalls, cooking lessons, etc.

Motor Show December. Showcasing cars and motorbikes manufactured in the region and elsewhere.

New Year's Eve 31 December. DJ music, street food and the burning of an effigy ('Vecchione') herald the New Year.

EATING OUT

It is not for nothing that the city is known as 'Bologna la Grassa' ('the fat one'). The city has 41 products protected by the European DOP (Designazione d'Origine Protetta) – more than any other city in Italy – an abundance of excellent restaurants, a tradition of long and leisurely meals and a spiralling number of cooking schools where visitors can learn the secrets of the local cuisine. It is generally regarded as the culinary capital of Italy. *Tortellini* remains the city's signature pasta dish, confirmed by an annual international cookery contest to determine the finest creations.

⊙ PARMA – HAVEN OF GASTRONOMY

Crudo di Parma (Parma Ham and locally known as *prosciutto crudo*) and Parmigiano, the hard sharp-flavoured cheese, are intricately linked because the whey – the waste product from Parmigiano-Reggiano production – forms part of the quality fodder of the special pigs that produce Parma ham. True Parma ham is branded with the five-pointed crown of the medieval dukes of Parma and is produced in the Langhirino hills south of Parma. Here the raw hind thighs are hung in drying sheds for up to 10 months. The air that blows through the sheds is said to impart a sweet flavour to the meat – unlike cheap, mass-produced *prosciutto crudo* which is injected with brine and artificially dried to speed up the curing process. Try it as a starter, sliced into wafer-thin slivers for eating with bread, melon or figs. Superior Parmigiano-Reggiano, the king of Parmesans, is especially delicious with apples, pears or a good red wine. To meet the master cheese-makers and taste their products visit www.parmigiano-reggiano.it.

Tagliatelle al ragù

The regional cuisine is robust yet refined. Unless you fall for a tourist trap, it is a challenge to eat badly in Bologna and Emilia-Romagna in general. The quality of ingredients is superb and local people are so demanding that mediocrity is punished. In the wealthy agricultural region of Emilia-Romagna each town produces its own pasta dishes and signature foods. Modena jealously guards the secrets of its world-renowned artisanal vinegar, Parma has patented Parmesan cheese and Italy's favourite ham *(prosciutto crudo di Parma)* and the Ferrara area can only mean *cappellacci di zucca*, pumpkin-stuffed pasta, or *salama da sugo*, pig's liver and tongue stuffed into a pig's bladder and cured in wine.

The region is a trailblazer in food and wine routes *(Strade dei Vini e dei Sapori)*. While these trails are often more of a promotional tool than a genuine excuse to tickle your taste buds, they are a convenient way to track down the top local producers of anything from asparagus to Parma ham and Parmesan cheese.

WHERE TO EAT

With gastronomic treats on offer in the Mercato di Mezzo, the ancient heart of the city, it is tempting to have snacks on the run. Here one of the many delis will make you up a *padina* or *crescentina* (flat focaccia-like bread) with a generous filling of finely

Café life on Via Caprarie

sliced *prosciutto di Parma*, *mortadella* or *squacquerone* (fresh tangy cream cheese). Or you can choose from the enticing array of canapés and tapas-style food, including fish, in the covered Mercato di Mezzo, which can either be taken away or consumed at casual communal tables.

Main meals are served in a **ristorante**, **trattoria** or **osteria** but the difference between the three is negligible these days. An **osteria**, traditionally a tavern or inn serving wine and pasta, can nowadays range from traditional to trendy (eg Modena's Osteria Francescana was voted the world's best restaurant in 2018). A **pizzeria** often extends to pasta and meat dishes but usually serves proper pizza bubbling hot from a wood-fired brick oven. The Italians prefer to eat pizza in the evening, and to accompany it with beer rather than wine. An **enoteca** or wine bar boasts a serious selection of fine wines, many available by the glass, and often served with a platter of cheese or charcuterie. Many inns or bars also serve food, especially pasta, and often have late-opening hours.

As in the rest of Italy, restaurants offer four courses: *antipasti* (hors d'oeuvres), the *primo* (first course, typically pasta in Emilia-Romagna but also risotto or soup), the *secondo* (main course of fish or meat) and the *dolce* (dessert), followed perhaps by cheese, coffee and a *digestivo*. Not that you would be expected, these days, to wade through every course.

ANTIPASTI

The most characteristic antipasto is a platter of assorted *salumi* – cured pork products such as wafer-thin slices of *prosciutto crudo di Parma* (Parma ham), *mortadella*, *salami*, *coppa di testa* (brawn), *cíccioli* (pork from Parma) and, if you're lucky, *culatello di Zibello*, one of the most prized and expensive of Italy's *salumi*, produced around Zibello, south of Parma. *Salumi* might be accompanied by a slice of crumbly Parmigiano-Reggiano cheese. Vegetable anti-pasti are likely to feature *peperoni* (peppers), *zucchini* (courgettes), *melanzane* (aubergine or eggplant) and *carciofi* (artichokes).

⊙ FAR FROM BALONEY

If you think of *mortadella* as the pre-packaged, pre-sliced and over-processed cold cut (American 'bologna sausage' or 'balo-ney') from your local supermarket, think again. Eating Mortadella di Bologna in its birthplace is a completely different experience. The pork is carefully selected according to strict regulation im-posed by its PGI (Protected Geographical Indication), then finely ground and flavoured with small white flecks of high quality pork fat (from the neck of the pig), peppercorns and (sometimes) pista-chios. It is then heat-cured for a few hours or several days accord-ing to the size. Sausages are typically between 5.5kg and 6.5kg (12 and 14 lbs) though in 1989 one was made that was over 5.75m (19ft) long, and 1,300kg (2,864 lbs) in weight. *Mortadella* should be sliced as thinly as possible and eaten with fresh, crusty bread along with a glass of light fruity red wine; alternatively you can have it as an appetiser in small diced cubes, as a creamy mousse with antipasti or as a stuffing for Bologna's famous *tortellini*. So popular is the pink sausage that there is a food festival in Bologna devoted to it: the MortadellaBò in mid-October.

PRIMO

Tortellini, delicate parcels of pasta filled with pork, ham, *mortadella* and Parmesan cheese, is a tasty Bolognese speciality served typically *in brodo* (fragrant chicken broth) or simply with butter and Parmesan. Ideally the pasta will be handmade – you get 20 to 30 percent less filling if it's made with a machine. Other typical dishes are *tortellini* with ricotta and spinach and *tagliatelle* usually served with the true Bolognese sauce. *Ragù* is also used in the ubiquitous *lasagne*, another authentic dish of Bologna. Look out too for regional pastas such as *passatelli*, *cappelletti* ('little hats') or the bigger version: *cappellacci*, filled with pumpkin and Parmesan, and *anolini* ('rings') stuffed with beef, parmesan and breadcrumbs, and served in chicken broth.

SECONDI

Pork is the king of meats, served in variety of ways. Most menus will feature *cotellata alla bolognese*, a thin slice of pork (or veal cutlet) fried in breadcrumbs then baked with Parma ham and Parmesan cheese. *Bollito misto* (mixed boiled meats) is a stew of meats such as flank of beef, veal or ox tongue and Italian sausages, slowly simmered with celery, carrots and herbs and served with different sauces. *Fritto misto alla bolognese* is a mixed fry, varying from place to place but typically including potato croquettes, mozzarella, lamb, brains, zucchini, artichoke wedges, cauliflower florets and aubergine, all dipped in batter and deep fried. Some

Tagliatelle tresses

Tagliatelle's origins go back to the 1487 wedding feast of Lucrezia Borgia and the Duke of Ferrara. The chef chosen to produce the lavish banquet included a new type of pasta, shaped in long golden strips, to reflect the blond tresses of the bride.

restaurants offer fresh fish but meat dominates the main courses. One of the best and most affordable places for fish and seafood is Banco 32 in the Mercato delle Erbe, next to the fishmonger. The seating is basic but the fish is brilliantly fresh, and there's a buzzy atmosphere.

DOLCI

Desserts range from a fruit salad or *gelato* to a choice of elaborate home-made des-

Local mortadella for sale

serts and cakes. Traditional desserts are *zuppa inglese* (the trifle-like 'English soup'), *tiramisu*, and *torta di riso,* a cake of rice, sugar, almonds and milk. Don't be surprised if you are offered gelato with a drizzle of balsamic vinegar. This should be the very superior Aceto Balsamico Tradizionale di Modena. It tastes much sweeter than ordinary Balsamic vinegar and can be used in salads, drizzled over fresh berries or even with honey over Parmigiano-Reggiano cheese. Aceto Balsamico in its pricey artisanal version bears no resemblance to the industrial liquid found in supermarkets.

GELATI

Greedy Bologna naturally excels at ice cream. As an alternative to a restaurant dessert you could do as many Bolognesi do and buy an ice cream from one of the superb *gelaterie*. The Bolognesi invariably disagree on which is best but firm favourites are **Sorbetteria Castiglione**, Via Castiglione 44

Spag Bol?

It may seem surprising but one dish you won't find in Bologna is spaghetti bolognese The *ragù alla bolognese*, which in its home town is a rich chunky blend of minced pork and beef, veg, wine, whole milk and tomato, is used to dress *tagliatelle*, never spaghetti.

d/e, **Gelateria Ugo**, Via San Felice 24, **Gelatauro**, Via San Vitale 98 and **Cremeria Cavour** in Piazza Cavour.

WINES

The well-deserved reputation for good living in Emilia Romagna is based more on food than wine. Huge amounts are produced but the quantity outweighs the quality. Nevertheless the wines have improved dramatically over the last two or three decades. Gone are the days of cheap, sweet, sparkling Lambrusco – at least in Italy. There are now some decent quality DOC dry (or off-dry), frothy Lambruscos with a pleasant acidity which goes well with the rich regional food. The Romagna side of the region, stretching east from Bologna to the coast, produces Sangiovese reds and the rather ordinary Trebbiano whites. Sangiovese varies enormously, from thin and tart to smooth dry, ruby red and full of flavour – but like Lambrusco it has seen a dramatic improvement. The best, such as Romagna DOC, competes with Italy's finest Sangiovese – and Sangiovese is Italy's most widely planted vine variety. Pignoletto, from the hills around Bologna and served throughout the city, is a delicate affordable white which goes well with antipasti and seafood. The sparkling form is a popular *aperitivo*.

Restaurants invariably offer wines from other regions, such as Barolo from Piedmont or Brunello from Tuscany, while gourmet restaurants will also list a smaller selection of international wines. House wine, *vino della casa*, is normally acceptable and always reasonably priced.

TO HELP YOU ORDER

A table for one/two/three **Un tavolo per una persona/per due/per tre**

I would like... **Vorrei...**

The bill, please. **Il conto, per favore**

I'd like a/an/some... **Vorrei...**

beer **una birra**	pepper **del pepe**
bread **del pane**	potatoes **delle patate**
butter **del burro**	salad **un'insalata**
coffee **un caffè**	salt **del sale**
fish **del pesce**	soup **una minestra**
fruit **della frutta**	sugar **dello zucchero**
ice cream **un gelato**	tea **un tè**
meat **della carne**	water **dell'acqua**
milk **del latte**	wine **del vino**

MENU READER

aglio garlic	**mela** apple
agnello lamb	**melanzane** aubergine
aragosta lobster	**merluzzo** cod
arancia orange	**ostriche** oysters
bistecca beefsteak	**pesca** peach
braciola chop	**pollo** chicken
carciofi artichokes	**pomodori** tomatoes
crostacei shellfish	**prosciutto** ham
fegato liver	**rognoni** kidneys
fiche figs	**tonno** tuna
formaggio cheese	**uovo** egg
frutti di mare seafood	**uva** grapes
funghi mushrooms	**verdure** vegetables
maiale pork	**vitello** veal
manzo beef	**vongole** clams

PLACES TO EAT

The price bands are based on a two-course meal including a glass of wine, service and cover charge.

€€€	over €40
€€	€30–€40
€	under €30

PIAZZA MAGGIORE AND AROUND

Ca' Pelletti € *Via Altabella 15 c/d; tel: 051-266 629; www.capellettilocandaita lia.it; Mon–Thu 8am–10pm, Fri 8am–11pm, Sat 9am–11pm, Sun 9am–10pm.* A busy little *locanda*, catering for all tastes all day: lavish breakfasts (served until noon), lovely cakes, local pasta dishes (including vegetarian), *prosciutto*, salads and sweet and savoury *piadine* (sandwiches). Take-away also available. Informal setting and welcoming atmosphere.

Da Gianni €€ *Via Clavature 18; tel: 051-229 43; www.trattoria-gianni.it; closed all day Mon and Sun pm and August.* Tucked down an alley in the 'foodie' quarter near San Petronio, this is one of Bologna's best trattorias, popular with both locals and tourists-in-the-know. Menus are in Italian only but staff will help you choose from the Bolognese dishes. Try the melt-in-the-mouth *tortellini in brodo*, the *tagliatelle* or *gnocchi* with *ragù Bolognese* and the *bollito misto* (boiled meats – better than it sounds).

Eataly €–€€€ *Via degli Orefici 19; tel: 051-095 2820; www.eataly.it; Mon–Sat 8am–11.30pm, Sun 10am–11.30pm.* Part of the successful Eataly emporium, this is set inside a large bookshop with a variety of eating and drinking places on different floors. Excellent quality and choice and a popular spot for cocktails.

Enoteca Storica Faccioli €–€€ *Via Altabella 15b; mobile: (0039) 349 3002939; Mon, Wed–Fri noon–3pm, 5–10pm, Tue 5–10pm, Sat 11am–10pm, Sun noon–3pm, 5–9pm.* An historic, up-market wine bar with food, this place puts wine on a pedestal while serving unpretentious, genuine food, from cold cuts and cheeses to *crostini*, *lasagne* and *tortellini*.

Fior di Sale €€ *Via Altabella 11d; tel: 051-281 2980; Tue–Sat 12.30–3pm, 6.30pm–midnight, Sun 11am–8pm.* This small but smart restaurant serves up Italian classics with a contemporary flair, accompanied by a wide selection of excellent Italian wines.

Pappagallo €€€ *Piazza della Mercanzia 3c; tel: 051-232 807; www.alpappagallo.it; open daily.* The Parrot (Pappagallo) is a charming old-world institution with fine dining, formal service and autographed photos of the many celebrities who have dined here (Sophia Loren, Gina Lollobrigida, Alfred Hitchcock, Frank Sinatra, Sharon Stone – just to name a few). The menu sticks strictly to Bolognese cuisine. If you haven't tasted the local *tortellini in brodo,* make this the place to try it. Reservations recommended.

Rodrigo €€€ *Via della Zecca 2h; tel: 051-235 536; www.ristoranterodrigobologna.it; closed Sun.* In a palazzo formerly occupied by the National Mint, this is a long-established restaurant known for home-made pasta, fresh fish and variety of *funghi* in season (*porcini, chiodini, finferli* and more). Excellent choice of wines.

Trattoria Battibecco €€€ *Via Battibecco 4; tel: 051-223 298; www.battibecco.com; closed Sat lunch and Sun.* Splash out on creative dishes such as pumpkin and ginger risotto with marinated duck breast or lamb in pistachio crust with caramelised yellow onion; there are also Bolognese specialities, a good choice of fish and an excellent wine list. Tucked in an alley, close to Piazza Maggiore, it has a smart, stylish interior and professional staff. Popular with locals, reservations recommended.

EAST OF PIAZZA MAGGIORE

Clorofilla € *Strada Maggiore 64c; tel: 051-235 343; closed Sun.* Bucking the Bolognese trend, the motto here is 'Eat your way to good health' and the dishes in this simple, wood-panelled restaurant are the perfect antidote to the rich and calorific local cuisine. Expect seitan steaks, couscous, tofu, vegetable drinks, vegan dishes and diverse salads.

Grassilli €€€ *Via dal Luzzo 3; tel: 051-222 961;* www.ristorantegrassilli. weebly.com; *closed all day Wed and Sun pm*. Close to the Two Towers this is an elegant and upmarket restaurant with the feel of an exclusive club. It was founded in 1944 and the many black and white photos (Luciano Pavarotti and Placido Domingo among them) recall the times when it was a popular haunt of opera singers. The cuisine is primarily Bolognese, but with a few French touches. Limited seating, booking recommended.

Scaccomatto €€€ *Via Broccaindosso 63; tel: 051-263 404;* www.ris torantescaccomatto.com; *closed Mon lunch*. If heavy Bolognese cuisine is taking its toll try Mario Ferrara's lighter dishes from southern Italy. He hails from Basilicata and founded the restaurant in 1987, bringing to the heart of Bologna an almost unheard of cuisine. His artfully-presented and often innovative dishes have proved very popular. Expect five- and six-course fish, meat or vegetable tasting menus.

UNIVERSITY QUARTER

Cantina Bentivoglio € *Via Mascarella 4b; tel: 051-265 416;* www.cantinaben tivoglio.it; *daily 8pm–2am, closed Sun in summer and all of August*. Set in the lively university quarter this trusty tavern occupies the wine cellar of the Palazzo Bentivoglio. For over 50 years locals of all ages have been coming to soak up the live jazz, sound Bolognese food and informal atmosphere.

Trattoria/Pizzeria delle Belle Arti € *Via delle Belle Arti 14; tel: 051-225 581;* www.belleartitrattoriapizzeria.com; *open daily for lunch and dinner*. A family-run rustic trattoria serving local dishes as well as fish and paella, Calabrian cuisine and good pizzas from the wood-fired oven. Al fresco meals on the veranda in summer.

NORTH AND WEST OF PIAZZA MAGGIORE

Al Cambio €€–€€€ *Via Stalingrado 150; tel: 051-328 118;* www.ris torantealcambio.it; *closed Sun*. Set outside the city walls, close to the Fiera district, this gastronomic temple serves Bolognese favourites with a creative twist. It is popular with local gourmets and foodie tourists in the know. Smart setting, professional service.

Altro? € *Mercato delle Erbe, Via Ugo Bassi 23–25, tel: 351-014 4191; www.al trobologna.com, Mon–Fri 8am–11.30pm, Sat 8am–1am.* Within the Mercato delle Erbe this is a new concept of a dozen or so outlets offering an array of high-quality simple food, sourced from the market: delicious pizza, veggie snacks, fish dishes, soups and salads. There is waiter service for lunch and dinner when there is more substantial fare on offer, otherwise it's self-service. At night it transforms to a cool spot for *aperitivos.*

Caminetto d'Oro €€ *Via de'Falegnami 4; tel: 051-263 494; www.caminet todoro.it; closed Sun.* This long-established family-run restaurant rustles up fine steaks and delicious desserts. Ingredients are market-fresh and the bread and pasta is made in-house. There's also a well-stocked wine cellar. Very popular, especially in the evenings, so book ahead.

Dal Biassanot €–€€ *Via Piella 16a; tel: 051-230 644; www.dalbiassanot.it; open daily.* Next door to the 'secret window' overlooking a canal, this is a warm, welcoming and very popular trattoria with top-notch local cuisine. Watch the *sfolgina* (pasta lady) rolling and cutting the pasta into perfect little shapes, then tuck into mouthwatering *tortellini rosa con pinoli e prosciutto* (pink tortelloni with pine nuts and Parma ham) or *tortelloni di ricotta burro e salvia* (with butter and sage), followed perhaps by roast rabbit or wild boar. If any space left, indulge in the chocolate cake with mascarpone cream.

Da Pietro €–€€ *Via de'Falegnami 18a; tel: 051-648 6240; www.trattoria dapietro.it; closed Sun.* This welcoming, award-winning, family-run trattoria serves Bolognese, Emilian and Umbrian dishes from home-made pasta to grills, with truffles and mushrooms in season. Summer terrace.

Del Rosso € *Via Augusto Righi 30; tel: 051-236 730; www.trattoriadelros so.com; open daily lunch and dinner.* Between Via dell'Indipendenza and the university quarter, this is a cheap and unpretentious trattoria serving authentic Bolognese fare. Try the *crescentine* (savoury fried bread) with Parma ham, *mortadella* or *squacquerone* (fresh and tangy cream cheese) and wash it down with *vino sfuso* (wine on tap).

Ex Forno €–€€ *MAMbo, Via Don Minzoni 14e; tel: 051-649 3896; www. exforno.com, Tue–Thu 7am–1am, Fri 7am–2am, Sat 10am–2am, Sat*

10am–1am. Come to see the art crowd in the modern MAMbo museum (see page 66). Decor combines vintage with the chic and contemporary. Daily specials, sumptuous salads, raw meats and fish are served at lunchtime, but it's particularly popular for the cocktails and the excellent *aperitivo* buffet (served from 7pm) with the likes of *crescente* (focaccia-style bread), couscous and tempura vegetables. Sundays are very popular for brunch.

Franco Rossi €€€ *Via Goito 3; tel: 051-238 818;* www.ristorantefran corossi.it; *closed Sun.* Set just off busy Via dell'Indipendenza, this elegant and intimate spot serves classic Bolognese and Emilian cuisine with a lighter and creative touch. Choice of meat or fish menus, and a fine wine list.

Le Stanze €–€€ *Via Borgo San Pietro 1; tel: 051-228 767;* www.lestanze cafe.it; *Tue–Sun 11am–1am.* A bizarre but fashionable bar-restaurant set in a deconsecrated chapel in the Bentivoglio palace. The food is fine but cannot compete with the frescoes.

Serghei €€ *Via Piella 12; tel: 051-233 533; closed Sat and Sun.* Set in the city's secretive 'canal street', this homely Bolognese trattoria is strong on pasta dishes, especially *tortellini* and *tortelloni in brodo.* Popular too for cocktails.

Trattoria Da Me €–€€ *Via San Felice 50A; tel: 051-555 486; closed Mon and Sun dinner.* Previously Da Danio, this historic and homely trattoria was reopened in 2016 by Elisa, granddaughter of the celebrated original owner Danio. Like her grandfather she produces authentic home-made Bolognese cuisine such as *tagliatelle al ragù, tortellini in brodo* and *cotoletta alla Bolognese* at affordable prices. Expect a warm welcome and a charming vintage setting.

Twinside €–€€ *Via de' Falegnami 6; tel: 051-991 1797;* https://twinside. net; *Mon–Sat 12.30–11.30pm.* Run by the owners of the neighbouring Caminetto d'Oro, this bistro, with an attractive modern interior, has tasty light modern Italian dishes along with Bolognese favourites. Beef tartare is a speciality, bread, pastry and ice-cream are all homemade. Excellent range of Italian wines by the glass.

SOUTH OF THE CENTRE

Biagi € *Via Saragozza 65; tel: 051-407 0049; www.ristorantebiagi1937. com; open Mon and Wed–Sat evenings, Sun also afternoons, closed Tues.* Near the Saragozza Gate this family-run restaurant, now in the third generation, has been welcoming clients since 1937. Come for authentic home-made Bolognese cuisine: *mortadella* mousse, *tortellini in brodo* or *tagliatelle al ragù*, followed perhaps by the *cotellata alla bolognese*, washed down with Sangiovese wine.

Drogheria della Rosa €€ *Via Cartoleria 10; tel: 051-222 529; www.droghe riadellarosa.it; open daily lunch and dinner.* One of Bologna's best-known trattorias, occupying an old pharmacy. The menu is short, the food simple but perfect. Classics include *tagliatelle* with *ragù* (meat sauce) and *tortelli* filled with *stracchino* and *squacquerone* cheeses with seasoned vegetables. Follow on with fillet steak in a dark sauce of Modena balsamic vinegar.

Osteria de' Poeti €€ *Via de' Poeti 1b; tel: 051-236 166; www.osteriade poeti.com; closed Mon.* This historic cellar-restaurant could be mistaken for a tourist trap but is equally popular with locals, enticed by the live music, the hearty regional cuisine and vast choice of wines. (Opt for the 'quiet room' if the music doesn't appeal). The Osteria acquired its name in the early 19th century when it was a popular haunt of poets and artists.

FERRARA

La Provvidenza €€ *Corso Ercole I d'Este 9; tel: 0532-205 187; www.ris torantelaprovvidenza.com; closed Mon and dinner on Sun.* This leading restaurant has a gentrified rustic interior and offers a range of Ferrara specialities, from *pasticcio ferrarese* (pasta with a mushroom and meat sauce) to *fritto misto di carne* (mixed grill).

La Romantica €€ *Via Ripagrande 36; tel: 0532-765 975; www.trattorialaro mantica.com; closed Sun and Mon lunch.* A suitably romantic inn, set in the former stables of a 17th-century palace. Regional pasta dishes include *cappellacci di zucca*, with pumpkin, walnuts and sage; and *garganelli* with asparagus and mushrooms. Leave room for bangers-and-mash, Ferrara-style.

MODENA

Hosteria Giusti €€–€€€ *Via Farini 75; tel: 059-222 533*; www.hosteria giusti.it; *Tue–Sat lunch only*. This little gem at the rear of a famous deli favours meat, from roast suckling pig to cold cuts and fried *cotechino di Modena* (pork sausage) with *zabaglione* sauce. Delicious home-made pastas and desserts. It is rustic but elegant, and very welcoming.

Osteria Francescana €€€ *Via Stella 2; tel: 059-223 912*; www.osteriafrancesca na.it; *Tue–Sat lunch and dinner*. The brainchild of master chef Massimo Bottura, this Osteria has three Michelin stars and in 2016 and 2018 was voted the World's Best Restaurant. Expect experimental, deconstructed versions of Italian classics. Book a long time in advance and be prepared for a very hefty bill.

PARMA

La Greppia €€–€€€ *Strada Garibaldi 39a; tel: 0521-233 686*; www.lagrep piaparma.it; *lunch and dinner daily*. This elegant city-centre gastronomic temple creates the very best of Parma-style cuisine, from *tortelli di erbette*, vegetable-stuffed pasta, to *culatello di Zibello*, the prized cured meat.

Trattoria del Tribunale €–€€ *Vicolo Politi 5; tel: 0521-285 527*; www.trat toriadeltribunale.it; *lunch and dinner daily*. A welcoming and central but hard-to find inn that serves *tortellini* stuffed with pumpkin and herbs, or ricotta and spinach, naturally coated in Parmesan.

RAVENNA

Ca'De Ven € *Via Corrado Ricci 24; tel: 0544-30163*; www.cadeven.it; *Tue–Sun lunch and dinner*. As 'the house of wine' this quirky palazzo, with long communal tables, serves good regional wines with tasty rustic fare based on *piadine* (flat bread), cold cuts, cheese and, for dessert, caramelised figs.

La Gardela €–€€ *Via Ponte Marino 3; tel: 0544-217 147*; www.ristorante lagardela.com; *Fri–Wed lunch and dinner*. This friendly inn specialises in meat and fish grills as well as vegetable pasta dishes, including mushrooms and truffles in season. Summer terrace.

A-Z TRAVEL TIPS

A SUMMARY OF PRACTICAL INFORMATION

A

ACCOMMODATION

Bologna has seen an increasing number of hotels and B&Bs in recent years, particularly those catering for tourists. However during the major trade fairs the accommodation is never sufficient and booking well in advance is crucial. Unless you are going specifically for a fair, these times are best avoided altogether, especially as hotel prices double or even treble. The main fairs are **Cosmoprof** (Cosmetics) in March, **Fiera del Libro per Ragazzi** (Children's Book Fair) in early April, **Cersaie** (ceramics) in late September and **Saie** (for the building industry) in mid-November. Finding a hotel room in the historic centre at other periods is generally not a problem. The quietest periods are the second week of January, February and mid-summer when it's very hot and many Bolognesi leave the city. Some restaurants may be closed for a couple of weeks or more in August.

Bologna has plenty of upmarket business hotels, many on the periphery of the city, but to have a true sense of the city stay in the historic centre even if it may mean paying more. Particularly appealing are the four 'Art hotels' that have cornered the market in seductive boutique hotels, all family-run, intimate, romantic hideaways. All occupy atmospheric palaces in the pedestrianised part of town and provide bikes for guests free of charge.

The centre has a good choice of B&B accommodation. Quality and price often compare favourably with 3-star hotels and any lack of amenities are more than compensated for by the personal welcome and the intimacy of the setting. B&Bs in the historic centre tend to be very small so early booking is essential. If you arrive on spec the Bologna Welcome tourist office (www.bolognawelcome.com) will advise on available accommodation and will do the booking for you.

Prices vary depending on season and days of the week, as well as trade fairs. Substantial price reductions can be found in mid-winter, and also in July and August which are low season. Bear in mind however that locals tend to go away in August (though less so than previously) and quite a few restaurants are closed for a couple of weeks or more.

When making a reservation, a deposit of one night's stay, payable by credit card, is usually requested. Failure to inform the hotel in advance of cancellation will normally incur the loss of the deposit.

Beware of Bologna's tourist tax, introduced in 2012, which will add €1.50–5 per person per night to the cost of your room, depending on the rates. This has to be paid directly to your hotel at the end of your stay. Children under 14 are excluded from the tax.

> I'd like a single/double room/twin beds **Vorrei una camera singola/matrimoniale/due letti singoli**
> With bath/shower **con bagno/doccia**
> What's the rate per night? **Quanto costa per notte?**

AIRPORT

Bologna's Guglielmo Marconi Airport (www.bologna-airport.it) is a mere 6km (4 miles) northwest of the city centre and has easy access. The Aerobus-BLQ shuttle service (http://aerobus.bo.it) provides a regular link with the city centre and Bologna Central Station. It runs daily from 5.30am to 12.15am, departs every 11 minutes, takes around 30 minutes and costs €6 for a single journey. Tickets can be bought at vending machines at the airport or railway station, at TPER ticket offices or online. For the city centre alight at Via dei Mille, the next and last stop is Bologna Central Station. Another shuttle service is Vivara Green (www.vivaraviaggi.it) that connects the airport to city hotels and needs to be pre-booked. Online bookings are accepted until noon of the day before the service (you fill in times of flights, name of hotel and pay in advance). For late reservations tel: (00 39) 051 760 622. The cost is €8 one way and the transfer time is around 30 minutes. The service was suspended at the time of writing so check online.

Taxis from the airport to the central station cost around €20–25 to the city centre, slightly more at night and on Sundays. The taxis at the airport have meters but it is always wise to check first on the approximate cost of your journey.

Taxis: Cotabo, tel: 051-372 727; Radio Taxi, tel: 051-4590.

B

BICYCLE HIRE

In Bologna the uneven cobbled streets and ubiquitous pedestrian-only colonnades don't make for ideal cycling. Very few locals choose to cycle, even in the university quarter – a sharp contrast to Ferrara where cycling is a way of life. Bologna's historic centre is very compact and much of it pedestrianised, making it very easy to go by foot. But for those who prefer two wheels there is no shortage of bikes to hire. Walk 'n Ride by BIKEinBo (www.touremiliaromagna.it) charges €15 a day, €30 for three days (including helmet, locks, map and raincoat) and there is a delivery service with or without collection (€5 or €8 accordingly). L'Altra Babele at Via Gandusio 10 (www.laltrababele.it), close to Bologna Central Station, charges €10 a day. A valid ID and deposit are required and there is no delivery service.

Dynamo La Velostazione (https://dynamo.bo.it) organises guided and self-guided cycle tours in Bologna in English.

The tourist office has a leaflet of cycling trails around the city (or accessible at www.comune.bologna.it). A few hotels have free bikes for the use of guests.

BUDGETING FOR YOUR TRIP

Flights to Bologna with a low-cost carrier start at around €60 return from the UK in low season, but are more commonly €120–250 return. Expect to pay €20 per person in a youth hostel, €120 upwards for a decent double room with bath or €100 in a simple hotel or B&B. Typically a three-course meal with wine costs from €30–40; a sandwich with a drink and coffee €8, coffee €1.50–€2.50; an *aperitivo* with nibbles or buffet included €10. Drinks at the bar are often cheaper than those served at a table. A metro or tram ticket is €1.30 if bought in advance, €1.50 if bought on the bus (exact cash required). Museum entrance charges range from €3–12. Entrance to state museums is free for EU citizens under 18 or over 65; and there is free for all entrance to state and some other museums on the first Sunday of the month. Look out for free concerts in churches, also free outdoor performances in summer.

C

CAMPING

The Campeggio Città di Bologna at the Centro Turistico Città (Via Romita 12/4a, tel: 051-325 016, www.hotelcamping.com) is close to the Fiera District but surrounded by greenery. A regular bus service links it to Bologna Central Train Station. Bungalows and mobile homes are available, as well as a restaurant, large swimming pool in summer (free of charge) and fitness centre (paying).

CAR HIRE

Most of Bologna's centre is closed to private traffic (see Driving) but you may want to hire a car to visit other cities of Emilia Romagna. The best rates are usually found online. The major rental companies have outlets at Bologna's G. Marconi airport. Hiring a small car costs €15–50 a day depending on the season. The cost includes third-party liability and taxes, but excludes insurance excess. Drivers must present their own national driving licence or one that is internationally recognised.

CLIMATE

Spring, early summer and early autumn are the best seasons to visit the city. The climate is hot and humid in summer, though the Apennine range can bring welcome breezes. Winters tend to be cold and wet, often with snow (particularly January and February). Lack of wind in winter also leads to fog and mist, often with high levels of air pollution. But there are also plenty of sunny days. A bonus of Bologna is the civilised system of porticoes allowing you to cross the city protected from rain and excessive heat.

	J	F	M	A	M	J	J	A	S	O	N	D
C°	6	9	13	18	21	25	27	27	24	19	13	8
F°	43	48	55	65	69	77	80	80	75	66	55	46

CLOTHING

Apart from the summer months, when all you need is light, cool clothes, bring plenty of layers, an umbrella and raincoat and in winter a warm coat or anorak. A pair of comfortable walking shoes is essential as you'll probably spend most of your time on foot. When visiting churches cover shoulders and don't wear skimpy attire.

CRIME

Take precautions against pickpockets. Leave important documents and valuables in the hotel safe, and keep a firm hold of handbags especially in crowded public areas and on public transport. For insurance purposes theft and loss must be reported immediately to the police.

I want to report a theft **Vorrei denunciare un furto.**
My wallet/passport/ticket has been stolen **Mi hanno rubato il portafoglio/il passaporto/il biglietto**

D

DRIVING

Bologna is at the crossroads of major motorways and can be reached directly from many major Italian cities. The A1 from Milan turns south at Bologna towards Florence, Rome and Naples; the A13 runs north to Ferrara and Padua; the A14 connects Bologna to Rimini and other coastal resorts on the Adriatic. Unless you are visiting sites outside Bologna a car is a positive drawback. The centre, which is a maze of one-way streets, is a mainly limited traffic zone (a 'ZTL') from 7am to 8pm daily, with access only for residents and authorised vehicles. In the so-called T area (via Ugo Bassi, Via Rizzoli and Via dell'Independenza) all traffic – even public transport and taxis – is forbidden at weekends, from 8am on Saturday to 10pm on Sunday. Entrance to the ZTL area is electrically monitored. Visitors staying in the city centre are allowed access but must provide their hotel or B&B with the car registration number in advance of arrival. Fines are imposed for those entering without a permit.

Road assistance: tel: 116

Parking. You can park in the blue lines, where price and times depend on the zones. Payment can be made with a smartphone or mobile. A list of car parks can be found on the www.bolognawelcome.it website. If you are staying at a hotel or B&B in the centre you are allowed access but only by giving advance notice. Hotels in the city centre with parking facilities charge around €30 a night.

Rules of the road. Drive on the right, overtake on the left. Unless otherwise indicated, speed limits are 50kmh (30mph) in towns and built-up areas, 90kmh (55mph) on main roads and 130kmh (80mph) on motorways (*austostrade*). Headlights must be kept on during the day on motorways and state roads (*strade statali*). Seat belts are compulsory in the front and back, and children should be properly restrained. The use of hand-held mobile phones while driving is prohibited. The blood alcohol limit is 0.05 percent, and police occasionally make random breath tests.

Breakdown. In case of accident or breakdown call 113 (General Emergencies) or, for the Automobile club of Italy (ACI) 803 116 free from landline or mobile with Italian provider or 02-6616 5593 or 06-491 115 from a mobile with a foreign provider. The ACI provides an efficient 24-hour service.

> Where's the nearest car park? **Dov'è il parcheggio più vicino?**
> Can I park here? **Posso parcheggiare qui?**
> Fill it up please **Faccia il pieno per favore**
> Unleaded/diesel **senza piombo/gasolio**
> I've had a breakdown **Ho avuto un guasto**
> There's been an accident **C'e stato un incidente**

E

ELECTRICITY
220V/50Hz AC is standard. Sockets take two-pin, round-pronged plugs. Visitors from the UK and the US will require an adaptor or transformer.

EMBASSIES AND CONSULATES
Australian Embassy, Via Antonio Bosio, 5, 00161 Rome, tel: 06-852 721, http://italy.embassy.gov.au
Canadian Embassy, Via Zara 30, 00198 Rome, tel: 06-854 441; www.canadainternational.gc.ca
Irish Embassy, Villa Spada, Via Giacomo Medici 1, 00153 Roma, tel: 06-585 2381; www.dfa.ie/irish-embassy/italy
Honorary consulate of South Africa, Via degli Agresti, 2, 40123 Bologna, tel: 051-272 600, http://lnx.sudafrica.it
Embassy of New Zealand, Via Clitunno, 44, 00198 Rome, tel: 06-853 7501, www.mfat.govt.nz/en/countries-and-regions/europe/italy/new-zealand-embassy

British Embassy, Via XX Settembre 80/a, 00187 Rome, tel: 06-4220 0001, www.gov.uk/government/world/organisations/british-embassy-rome
US Embassy, Via Vittorio Veneto 121, 00187 Rome, tel: 06-46741, https://it.usembassy.gov

EMERGENCIES
Police 112, **Fire** 115, **Ambulance** 118, **General Emergency** 113

G

GETTING TO BOLOGNA

Bologna is well connected to the major cities of Europe. From the UK direct flights to Bologna are operated by British Airways (www.britishairways.com) who fly from London Heathrow, easyJet (www.easyjet.com) from London Gatwick and Ryanair (www.ryanair.com) from Stansted, London Luton, Edinburgh and Manchester. Flight costs vary according to the time of year and day of the week. An off-season return booked in advance with a low-cost carrier can be as little as €60 (hand-luggage only).

American Airlines (www.aa.com) operate the only direct flights (June–Sept) from North America (Philadelphia) to Bologna. Otherwise there are many indirect flights with a change at one of the European hubs (Rome, Milan, Paris, Frankfurt or Zurich).

GUIDES AND TOURS

Two-hour walking tours of the city depart daily from the Bologna Welcome tourist office in Piazza Maggiore. In Italian and English, the guided tours take in the Basilica of San Petronio, the ancient market area, the Two Towers and other cultural highlights of the historic centre. (€15 per person and free for children under 12).

Bologna Welcome offers a host of other guided tours, both within the city and in the province of Emilia Romagna. Many of these are gastro-themed, eg the food stores of the medieval market, Sangiovese wine tours, a visit to a Parmigiano Reggiano cheese factory, a truffle factory or a tour of Modena's prestigious balsamic vinegar production. Motor aficionados can test drive a Ferrari, visit the two Ferrari museums and see the Ducati and Lamborghini factory floors and historical collections.

Il Salotto di Penelope (www.ilsalottodipenelope.it) is one of the city's 25 cookery schools where you can learn the secrets of making Bolognese pastas and other Emilian specialities.

H

HEALTH AND MEDICAL CARE

All EU countries have reciprocal arrangements for reclaiming the costs of medical services. UK residents should obtain the EHIC (European Health Insurance Card), available from post offices or online at www.gov.uk/european-health-insurance-card. This does not cover emergency repatriation costs or additional expenses. To cover all eventualities a travel insurance policy is advisable, and for non-EU residents essential. When/if the UK leaves the EU, check the new regulations in place. For insurance claims keep all receipts for medical treatment and any medicines prescribed.

The water is safe to drink but most locals drink mineral water.

If you need a doctor (*medico*), ask at a pharmacy or your hotel. For serious cases or emergencies dial 118 for an ambulance or head for the *Pronto Soccorso* (Accident and Emergency) of the local hospital which will also deal with emergency dental treatment.

Pharmacies. A pharmacy is identified by a green cross. Locations of pharmacies which are open after-hours are posted on all pharmacy doors. An all-night service is available at the Farmacia Comunale at Piazza Maggiore 6 in the centre of the city.

I need a doctor/dentist **Ho bisogno di un medico/dentista**
Where is the nearest chemist? **Dov'è la farmacia più vicina?**

L

LGBTQ TRAVELLERS

Bologna has a long tradition of openness towards diversity and minorities. Even in the 1970s, when very few Italian towns had openly gay-friendly bars or clubs, there were meeting places in the city for the LGBTQ community; and in 1995 Marcello Di Folco was elected Municipal Councillor of Bologna – the first transsexual in Europe to hold public office. The Igor Libreria, Via Santa Croce 10 (at the Senape Vivaio Urbano, www.senapevivaiourbano.com), is entirely devoted to LGBTQ culture.

The city is the seat of Arci Gay, Italy's biggest gay-rights organisation at Via Don Minzoni 18, tel: 051-095 7241, www.arcigay.it. This is also home to the Cassero LGBT Centre, the provincial branch of Arci Gay Cassero LGBT Centre (www.cassero.it) and venue of Il Cassero, one of the city's most popular LGBTQ clubs.

LGBTQ information, including services, associations and gay-friendly bars and clubs, can be found on the tourist information website (www. bolognawelcome.com).

M

MAPS

The Bologna Welcome tourist office at the airport or in Piazza Maggiore supply a useful free and updated map of the city. You are unlikely to need anything more detailed but if you require maps for other cities or areas of Emilia Romagna you can find them at La Feltrinelli bookshop by the Due Torri.

MEDIA

Most hotels in Bologna will provide satellite TV, broadcasting 24-hour English-speaking news channels. The Italian state TV network, RAI (Radiotelevisione Italiana) broadcasts three channels, RAI 1, 2 and 3, and a huge number of private channels pouring out soaps, films and quiz shows. The state-run radio stations (RAI 1, 2 and 3) mainly broadcast news, chat and music.

The *Bologna Press* (www.bolognapress.com) is an English-language online newspaper all about Bologna life, culture, business, economy and politics. Alternatively details of events are available on the Bologna Welcome website, www.bolognawelcome.com.

National dailies such as the *Corriere della Sera* and *La Repubblica* have Bologna sections, and Il *Resto del Carlino* (www.ilrestodelcarlino. it) is almost entirely devoted to Bologna, including listings (in Italian). The main English and foreign newspapers are available on the day of publication from major newsstands.

MONEY MATTERS

Currency. In common with most other European countries, the official currency used in Italy is the euro (€), divided into 100 cents. Euro notes come in denominations of 500, 200, 100, 50, 20, 10 and 5; coins come in denominations of 2 and 1, then 50, 20, 10, 5, 2 and 1 cents.

Exchange facilities. Banks offer the best rates, followed by exchange offices (*cambi*) and hotels. Some exchange offices offer commission-free facilities, but check that the exchange rate is not exorbitant. They are usually open Mon–Sat 8.30am–7.30pm. Both the airport and railway station have exchange offices.

Credit cards and cash machines. The major international credit cards are accepted in the majority of hotels, restaurants and stores.

I want to change some pounds/dollars **Desidero cambiare delle sterline/dei dollari**
Can I pay with a credit card? **Posso pagare con la carta di credito?**

O

OPENING TIMES

Banks generally open Monday–Friday 8.30am–1.30pm and 2.30–4pm, but hours vary; some open continuously from 8am–4pm.

Museums and art galleries. Opening times vary but closing day is nearly always Monday. Some museums close over the lunch period or close early, eg at 2pm or 3pm. The tourist office on Piazza Maggiore has up-to-date lists of opening hours for museums, galleries and churches.

Churches usually close from noon to 3pm or later, though San Petronio is open all day.

Shops are open Monday to Saturday, and many are also open on Sundays. Opening hours are traditionally 9am–1pm and 3.30–7.30pm but many shops are now open all day. Some shops close for at least a part of August.

P

POLICE

The city police or *Polizia Urbana* regulate traffic and enforce laws while the *Carabinieri* are the armed military police who handle law and order. In an emergency the Carabinieri (Via dei Bersaglieri 3) can be reached on 112 – or you can ring the general emergency number, 113. In the case of stolen goods, contact the Questura (police station) at Piazza Galileo 7, tel: 051-640 1111.

See also Emergencies.

Where's the nearest police station? **Dov'è il posto di polizia più vicino?**

POST OFFICES

The central post office, at Piazza Minghetti 4, is open Mon–Fri

8.20am–7.05pm, Sat 8.20am–12.35pm. Most other post offices open Mon–Fri 8.20am–1.35pm, Sat 8.20am–12.35pm. Stamps can be purchased at any post office but it is faster and easier to buy them from a *tabaccheria*.

> Where's the nearest post office? **Dov'è il l'ufficio postale più vicino?**
> I would like a stamp for this letter/postcard **Desidero un francobollo per questa lettera/cartolina**

PUBLIC HOLIDAYS

1 January *Capodanno* New Year's Day
6 January *Epifani (La Befana)* Epiphany
25 April *Festa della Liberazione* Liberation Day
1 May *Festa dei lavoratori* Labour Day
2 June *Festa della Repubblica* Republic Day
15 August *Ferragosto* Assumption
4 October *San Petronio*
1 November *Ognissanti* All Saints' Day
8 December *L'Immacolata Concezione* Immaculate Conception
25 December *Natale* Christmas Day
26 December *Santo Stefano* St Stephen's Day
Moveable dates:
Pasqua Easter
Lunedì di Pasqua Easter Monday

T

TELEPHONES

When phoning abroad, dial the international code, followed by the city or area code and then the number. Note that telephone numbers within Italy are usually 9 or 10 digits long but can be any amount of digits from

6–11. Numbers beginning with 800 are free. Italian area codes are incorporated into the numbers, so even if calling within Bologna you must include the code.

At the time of writing there are no mobile phone roaming charges for UK travellers to EU countries, however this is all subject to change post-Brexit; check before travelling. Some mobile phones need to be activated with a roaming facility or be 'unblocked' for use abroad. If you are in Italy for some time it's worth purchasing an Italian SIM 'pay as you go' (*scheda pre-pagata*) available from any mobile shop in Italy. To do so you will need your passport or ID card.

TIME ZONES

Italy is one hour ahead of Greenwich Mean Time (GMT). From the last Sunday in March to the last Sunday in October, clocks are put forward by one hour.

The chart below shows times across the globe when it is midday in Bologna.

New York	London	**Bologna**	Jo'burg	Sydney
6am	11am	**noon**	1pm	8pm

TIPPING

A 10 percent service charge is normally included in the restaurant bill and a tip on top of this is not expected. Most restaurants still impose an outdated cover and bread charge (*pane e coperto*) of around €1.50–5. For quick service in bars leave a coin or two with your till receipt when ordering. Taxi drivers do not expect a tip but always appreciate a bit extra.

Thank you, this is for you **Grazie, questo è per lei**
Keep the change **Tenga il resto**

TOILETS

The train and bus stations have public toilets, so does the Biblioteca Salaborsa on Piazza di Nettuno right in the centre. Otherwise it is generally a case of using the facilities of a café or bar. To avoid embarrassment, remember that *Signori* is Men, *Signore* is Women.

> Where are the toilets, please? **Dov'è sono i gabinetti, per favore?**

TOURIST INFORMATION

Italian Tourism authority offices abroad:

Australia: Level 2, 140 William Street, East Sydney NSW 2011, tel: 02-9357 2561

Canada: 365 Bay Street, Suite 503, Toronto (Ontario) M5H 2V1, tel: 416-925 4882

UK: 1 Princes Street, London W1B 2AY, tel: 020-7408 1254

US: **New York**: 686 Park Avenue, 3rd Floor, New York, NY 10065, tel: 212-245 5618

Los Angeles: 10850 Wilshire Blvd, Suite 575, Los Angeles, CA 90024, tel: 310-820 1898.

The common website for all tourist offices is www.enit.it.

Bologna Tourist Offices

The main Bologna Welcome tourist office (tel: 051-658 3111, open Mon–Sat 9am–7pm, Sun 10am–5pm) is in the heart of the city under the portico of Palazzo Podestà in Piazza Maggiore. Services include hotel booking, restaurant reservation, bookings for guided tours or tickets for flights, trains, theatre, cultural and sporting events. Staff are efficient and helpful and can supply free maps and leaflets in English. There is a second Bologna Welcome Office in the Arrivals' Hall of Bologna's G. Marconi airport and a third operates near the entrance of FICO Eataly World in Via Paolo Canali 8. Bologna Welcome has an excellent, up-to-date website, www.bolognawelcome.com, which gives you everything you need to know for a stay in the city from descriptions of hotels, restaurants and museums to where to go for an *aperitivo* or how to use the buses. Use the search box to make the most of it. The Bologna Welcome Card, available at both Bologna Welcome offices, allows you free admission to many museums plus discounts at numerous restaurants and shops. It is good value at €25 (Bologna Welcome Card Easy) or €40 (Bologna Welcome Card Plus).

The Mibac Call centre (Ministry of Cultural Heritage and Activities) is available in English, Spanish and Italian, free phone: 800 99 11 99.

TRANSPORT

The historic centre, where virtually all the attractions are located, is compact, flat and easily covered on foot. It is easy to find your way around with a free map from the tourist office, colonnades giving shelter from the elements and towers providing useful landmarks.

Bus. Bologna has a good public transport network run by TPER (www.tper.it) and covering the whole city and beyond. Routes and timetables are available on the TPER website. Tickets can be bought in advance from tobacconists, newsstands or from one of the five TPER information points in the city. A single ticket, which is valid for 75 minutes, costs €1.30 if bought in advance or €1.50 if bought on the bus (you need the exact change). Tickets bought before boarding must be validated as soon as you board the bus. A 24-hr ticket with unlimited bus travel costs €5, or a city pass for 10 journeys costs €12 and can be used by more than one person.

The coach station is located just 100m/yards from Bologna Central Train Station. Coach services connect Bologna with main Italian cities though trains tend get you there faster.

The City Red Bus (www.cityredbus.com) is an open-top bus operating daily, with an audioguide providing information en route in eight languages. 'Stop and Go' tickets are valid all day. The Bologna Welcome office in Piazza Maggiore sells tickets; alternatively you can buy them on board or at affiliated stores and hotels. The same company also runs the San Luca Express that connects the centre to the Basilica of San Luca, in season only. The Red City Bus tour and the San Luca Express are included in the Bologna Welcome Card Plus.

Rail. Bologna central train station (Piazza Medaglie d'Oro 2, www. bolognacentrale.it) is a key hub in the Italian rail network with high-speed trains connecting the city to Florence (30 minutes), Milan (one hour), Venice (1.5 hours) and Rome (2.5 hours). Trains are also the most efficient means of transport to cities of Emilia Romagna: Modena, Ferrara, Parma, Rimini and Ravenna. For complete online timetables and booking (in English or Italian) contact www.trenitalia.com.

The station is located about 20 minutes' walk from the historic centre on the northern edge of the city. There are two main train companies, Trenitalia and Italo (www.italotreno.it), both offering trains out of Bologna Centrale. The ticket office is open 6am–9pm; alternatively you can purchase tickets online or at the self-service vending machines. Tickets must be validated at the yellow machines in the station. If you have a return ticket you must validate it twice (once going, once returning).

Taxis. Taxis cannot be hailed in the street. The main ranks are at Bologna Central Station and Piazza Maggiore but there are others scattered through the city. Taxis have meters but it is always wise to agree an approximate cost with the driver before setting off. The fare will depend on the time of day, the day of the week and the number of pieces of luggage.

The following radio taxi companies offer a 24-hour service:
Cotabo: 051-372 727
Cat: 051-4590
Cosepuri Auto Blu: 051-519 090

When's the next bus/train to...? **Quando parte il prossimo autobus/treno per...?**
single (one-way) **andata**
return **andata e ritorno**
What's the fare to..? **Qual'è la tariffa per...?**

TRAVELLERS WITH DISABILITIES

Cobblestones and stairways within palazzi are disincentives for travellers with disabilities but there is now access in most public buildings and main museums. The Bologna Welcome website (www.bolognawelcome.com/en/for-disabled-visitors) has useful information for the disabled such as public and private transportation, free parking, accommodation, restaurants and useful links. The office also provides a handy map, *Bologna, A City for Everybody*, which marks routes for travellers with disabilities including written itineraries with full details of the easiest access, where to find lifts, etc. A special Radio-Taxi service (tel: 051-372 727) operates 24 hours for those in wheelchairs or those who need special assistance. Vehicles serving disabled persons can circulate in the ZTL (Restricted Traffic Zone) provided notice of the registration number can be given to the hotel or B&B in advance to pass on to the Municipality. In the case of access which is not previously communicated, details can be sent within 48 hours of entering the ontrolled area. Information in Italian only is available on the website of the Settore Mobilità, www.comune.bologna.it/trasporti. Vehicles used for the disabled are not subject to parking fees.

AccessiBol is an app to find accessible places in Bologna – with useful links. Alternatively contact Accessible Italy (www.accessibleitaly.com), a non-profit making organisation that helps foreign tourists with disabilities to plan their holidays in Italy.

V

VISAS AND ENTRY REQUIREMENTS

EU citizens need only a valid passport. Citizens of the US, Canada, Australia and New Zealand can stay for up to three months without a visa, and can extend their stay with a visa from the Italian embassy or consulate.

W

WEBSITES AND INTERNET ACCESS

www.bolognawelcome.com – official city tourist website, packed with information.

www.bologna-airport.it – Bologna airport information.

www.trenitalia.com – train information.

www.tper.it – bus information.

www.emiliaromagnaturismo.it – official website for the whole region, in both Italian and English with useful links.

www.cittadarte.emilia-romagna.it – for all the region's art cities.

www.turismo.comune.parma.it – Parma tourist information.

www.ferrarainfo.com – Ferrara tourist information.

www.visitmodena.it – Modena tourist information.

www.turismo.ra.it – Ravenna tourist information.

www.visit-rimini.com – Rimini tourist information.

To find free WiFi hotspots (indoor and outdoor) go to the Iperbole Wireless Network website (www.comune.bologna.it/wireless). The map is constantly updated.

In the city centre the tourist office on Piazza Maggiore, the archaeological museum and the Biblioteca Salaborsa are all WiFi hotspots.

Hotels generally include WiFi in the room rates. An increasing number of cafés and restaurants provide WiFi, with purchase of food or a drink, especially in the university quarter.

YOUTH HOSTELS

The best hostel is the **Ostello We_Bologna**, Via de' Carracci 69/14, hello@we-bologna.it or www.hostelworld.com, tel: 051-039 7900, a highly-rated design hostel 800m/yards northwest of the station. Rooms which accommodate two or four people all come with en suite bathroom and air conditioning. Communal areas include kitchen, breakfast and lounge, video room and outdoor area. 24-hour reception, free WiFi. Prices from €25 per person, breakfast is included.

RECOMMENDED HOTELS

Bologna has a wide range of accommodation from the large modern hotels on the periphery aimed at business travellers to the smaller hotels and B&Bs in the historic centre, which have far more appeal for tourists. Bologna is a city for all seasons but during the main trade fairs hotels can be booked up months in advance and prices double or often treble. Prices tend to fall in mid-summer and are generally at their cheapest in February, the quietest month. If you arrive without a reservation the Bologna Welcome tourist office (www.bolognawelcome.com) in Piazza Maggiore offers a free hotel-booking service.

Hotels are officially categorised from one-to-five stars, or, at the very top end of the scale, five-star deluxe. The stars assigned denote facilities (which sometimes don't exist) and are no real indicator of charm or atmosphere. The most prestigious hotel is undeniably the five-star deluxe Grand Hotel Majestic. Some of the most appealing hotels, right in the centre and integrating seamlessly into the medieval context, are the Bologna Art Hotels, a chain of three: The Commercianti, Orologio and Novecento (www.bolognarthotels.it). They also have a handful of centrally-located four- and five-star apartments available. B&Bs in Bologna are now plentiful but because of space restrictions in the city centre many of them only have one or two rooms.

Hotel rates usually include breakfast, though check first as a few hotels have started to charge it separately. Being Bologna, breakfast is usually a fairly substantial fare including a spread of fresh fruit, Parma ham, cheeses, yoghurts and freshly baked patisserie. If breakfast is not included in the room rate it is usually better value to pop out for a cappuccino and croissant in the local café.

As is the case in many of Italy's cities a tourist tax applies to any non-resident staying in a hotel or B&B. Children under 14 are exempt. The rate is €1.50–5 per person per night depending on the room rate, for up to a maximum of five nights. For a couple staying in a 4-star hotel for three nights there would be an extra cost of around €15. The tax must be paid to the hotel before departure (it is never paid in advance either to the hotel or to a tour operator or hotel website).

As a basic guide the symbols below indicate rack rates per night for standard double room including VAT, service and breakfast, but excluding tourist tax.

€€€€	over 300 euros
€€€	200–300 euros
€€	120–200 euros
€	under 120 euros

PIAZZA MAGGIORE AND AROUND

Art Hotel Commercianti €€-€€€ *Via de'Pignattari 11; tel: 051-745 7511*; www.art-hotel-commercianti.it. Set in a side street beside San Petronio, this frescoed medieval palace is home to a stylish yet seductive hotel in the very heart of the city. Well-restored public rooms lead to romantic bedrooms under the eaves, many of which have views across the alley to the Gothic windows of San Petronio or over the rooftops. Best rooms are at the top. Excellent buffet breakfast and free bikes.

Art Hotel Corona d'Oro 1890 €€–€€€ *Via Guglielmo Oberdan 12; tel: 051-745 7611*; www.hco.it. On a cobbled, traffic-free street close to the famous two towers, this delightful, peaceful hotel is one of the most sought-after city-centre retreats. An atmospheric medieval palazzo, it is said to have housed Italy's first printing works, and has been offering accommodation and a warm welcome since it first opened in 1890. A Renaissance portico, 16th-century coffered ceilings and the former winter garden, transformed into an elegant entrance hall, all add to the charm.

Art Hotel Novecento €€–€€€ *Piazza Galileo 4/3; tel: 051-745 7311*; www.bolognarthotels.it. A chic and glamorous designer hotel in Art Nouveau style right in the centre of the city. Guest rooms, which include suites, overlook historic corners of the medieval centre.

Art Hotel Orologio €€–€€€ *Via IV Novembre 10; tel: 051-745 7411*; www.bolognarthotels.it. This small, family-run, three-star hotel is much in demand for its unbeatable location beside Piazza Maggiore and for its old-world charm. Some rooms have views of the medieval Due Torri and the heart of historic Bologna.

Ca' Fosca Due Torri €€ *Via Caprarie 7; tel: 051-261 221; mobile: (00 39) 335 314761;* www.cafoscaduetorri.com. Set in the shadow of the medieval Due Torri this is a gem of a B&B, boasting a gracious Art Nouveau inspired interior and views of city towers and domes. Patrizia is a font of city knowledge and an exceptionally welcoming, extrovert and helpful hostess. Amenities include a library, guest kitchen and a winter garden where breakfast is served. Studios also available.

Cappello Rosso €€€€ *Via de Fusari 9; tel: 051-261 891;* www.alcappel lorosso.it. Luxury hotel in the centre, set in a former tavern that was renowned for its roast partridge. There are 33 rooms, each one different, but all contemporary, sleek and equipped with luxuries such as big-screen TVs and silk kimonos. Designer rooms include: the Silent Cage Room 4'33", dedicated to the American composer John Cage, the Shock in Pink room, which pays homage to Schiaparelli's surreal universe and Lettera 305, dedicated to the old Lettera 22 typewriter (with a gigantic keyboard on the ceiling).

Centrale € *Via della Zecca 2; tel: 051-006 3937;* www.albergocentralebo logna.it. One of Bologna's best two-star hotels: central, with clean and simple rooms in classic-style, excellent continental breakfast and staff who go out of their way to help. Rooms are on the third and fourth floor (with lift) of an 18th-century palazzo with fine views over the rooftops.

Delle Drapperie €–€€ *Via delle Drapperie 5; tel: 051-223 955;* www.alber godrapperie.com. Small and charming hotel in the heart of the bustling Mercato di Mezzo. Pretty rooms come in Art Nouveau style, all in different colours with lovely floral designs and antiques. Four junior suites overlook the rooftops.

Roma €€–€€€ *Via d'Azeglio 9; tel: 051-226 322;* www.hotelroma.biz. The location of the Roma is hard to beat: on a smart pedestrianised street, popular for shopping and *la passeggiata*, just a few steps from the Piazza Maggiore. The hotel has a civilised atmosphere, traditional rooms and personal service. Emilian specialities are served in the C'era Una Volta restaurant.

Torre Prendiparte €€€€ *Piazzetta Prendiparte; mobile: (00 39) 335 5616858; www.prendiparte.it.* A unique opportunity to rent your own 60m (197ft)-high medieval 900-year-old tower with a panoramic terrace (12 floors to climb). This is a romantic retreat – accommodation is for one couple only. The living areas with bedroom, kitchen and sitting room, take up three floors. All requirements are catered for including a private chef for a candlelit dinner. Popular for special occasions or a romantic and exclusive B&B for two. This unique experience comes of course with a high price tag.

UNIVERSITY QUARTER

Casa Ilaria € *Largo Respighi 8; tel: 051-412 4760; www.casailaria.com.* Very handy for the Teatro Comunale (main venue for opera, concerts and ballet), this is a quiet and welcoming B&B with spacious rooms and garden views. Tiziana is a gracious host and very helpful with information on the city and advice on local restaurants. Continental breakfasts come with delicious home-made cake – or there are eggs and bacon on request. The hosts also hold cookery courses and organise gourmet tours.

NORTH AND WEST

Allegro Italia Espresso €€ *Viale A. Masini 4/3; tel: 051-255 035;* www.al legroitalia.it. Design hotel with well-conceived rooms, chic public spaces and a fresh, contemporary feel. It's handy for the station but on a busy main road, 15–20 minutes' walk from Piazza Maggiore.

B&B Bologna nel Cuore €€ *Via Cesare Battisti 29; tel: 051-269 442;* www. bolognanelcuore.it. Expect a warm welcome and expert local knowledge from Maria Ketty, who has been running this B&B for 10 years. There are two attractively decorated and well-equipped double rooms and two apartments with cooking facilities.

B&B Galleria del Reno € *Via Marconi 51; mobile: (00 39) 346 2214121.* Simply furnished, affordable B&B enjoying views of the city centre. Very convenient location between the historic centre and the station. Free Wi-fi, tasty varied breakfast, but shared bathroom.

Cavour €–€€€ *Via Goito 4; tel: 051-228 111; www.cavour-hotel.com.* This friendly and professionally run three-star has an excellent location in a side street just off Via dell'Independanza, with plenty of good places to eat nearby. The 47 rooms vary in size and style from standard and superior to the newly furbished deluxe rooms, available with jacuzzi.

Grand Hotel Majestic €€€€ *Via dell'Indipendenza 8; tel: 051-225 445;* www.grandhotelmajestic.hotelsbologna.it. In a former 18th-century seminary, the hotel lives up to its name and provides a rendezvous for the most affluent Bolognese, many of whom come to dine in its prestigious restaurant I Carracci. Many a Hollywood legend has stayed here. Public rooms retain their former splendour: frescoed walls, moulded ceiling and grand chandeliers. Guest rooms combine classical charm and contemporary luxury and palatial suites are furnished with antiques and marble bathrooms with jacuzzis.

Il Guercino € *Via Luigi Serra; tel: 051-369 893; www.guercino.it.* This is a discreet, classic hotel in a quiet (although unfashionable) area 5 minutes' walk from the station, 20 plus to the historic centre. Rooms are comfortable and good value, though some are on the small side. Friendly, helpful staff and good breakfasts.

I Portici €€€–€€€€ *Via dell'Indipendenza 69; tel: 051-42185;* www. iporticihotel.com. This restored Art Nouveau palazzo is a four-star deluxe hotel and member of SLH group, Small Luxury Hotels of the World. The chic minimalist interior was the work of leading Italian and international designers. Guest rooms have parquet floors, pastel shades and, in the case of the deluxe rooms, original Art Nouveau frescoes. Rooms look out on to the park or Via dell'Indipendenza, a main shopping street. The I Portici Restaurant is one of the best in the city.

Metropolitan €€ *Via dell'Orso 6; tel: 051-229 393*; www.hotelmetropoli tan.com. The location between the city centre and the station combined with a fresh, contemporary Far Eastern decor make the Metropolitan a popular choice both for business travellers and tourists. Book well in advance for the cool new apartments at the top.

Royal Carlton €€€-€€€€ *Via Montebello 8; tel: 051-249 361*; www. royalhotelcarltonbologna.com. This austere-looking tower near the station contains a grand hotel with helpful staff, large comfortable bedrooms and hotel parking. The professional ambience and con- venient location five minutes' walk from the station and 10 from the historic centre make it a popular choice for executives and tour- ists alike. Inside the emphasis is on space, modern comforts and cool efficiency.

Touring €€ *Via De' Mattuiani 1; tel: 051-584 305*; www.hoteltouring.it. Friendly, family-run three-star hotel with a panoramic roof terrace look- ing onto the city and San Luca in the distance. Guest rooms vary from the older classic-style to the newly renovated contemporary rooms and spacious suites. In the summer months guests can enjoy the jacuzzi on the rooftop. Ten minutes' walk from Piazza Maggiore.

UNA Hotels Bologna Centro €€ *Viale Pietramellara 41/43; tel: 051- 60801*; www.gruppouna.it. Right in front of the station this is a modern design hotel and part of the Italian UNA chain. Chic, clean lines set off colourful panels and minimalist furniture makes for pleasantly un- cluttered rooms. Offers some good deals off season (but not during trade fairs).

SOUTH

Antica Casa Zucchini €€ *Via Santo Stefano 36; mobile: (00 39) 347 9110731*; www.anticacasazucchini.it. This charming B&B near the church of Santo Stefano occupies an historic house, parts of which date back to the mid-15th century. Features include a portico with Istrian stone capi- tals, grand 18th-century staircase and frescoed ceilings and antiques in the three bedrooms.

Il Convento dei Fiori di Seta €€ *Via Orfeo 34/4; tel: 051-221 697*; www.ilconventodeifioridiseta.com. Converted from a nunnery dating back to the 15th century, this little boutique hotel on the southern edge of the city has plenty of personality. Original features, such as vaulted rooms, frescoes and sacred altar sculptures have been retained but there's a nod to the modern era with chic contemporary lighting and seating, and mosaic tiled bathrooms. Four of the guest rooms have been fashioned out of the aisle and apse of the church, six are on the upper floor, individually designed in contemporary style.

Porta San Mamolo €€–€€€ *Vicolo Del Falcone 6/8; tel: 051-583 056*; www.hotel-portasanmamolo.it. This welcoming and very accommodating B&B is near the Porta San Mamolo on the southern edge of the city, 10–15 minutes' walk from the centre, with the advantage of a pretty courtyard garden for breakfasts in summer. Rooms, in traditional style (either doubles, triples or suites), are a good size and some have their own terrace.

Porta Saragozza € *Viale Carlo Pepoli 26; tel: 051-644 7437*; www.portasaragozza.it. This charming B&B retreat is set in a quiet residential zone just outside the city walls. The reception rooms are studded with antiques; the two bedrooms have a shared (but spacious and modern) bathroom. Talia Franceschini is a helpful (English- and French-speaking) hostess. Cash only.

Santo Stefano €–€€ *Via Santo Stefano 84; tel: 051-308 458*; www.bedandbreakfastsantostefano.com. This B&B by the Church of Santo Stefano wins many plaudits for its location and stylish contemporary design. The quietest guest rooms overlook the courtyard, and there are also well-equipped apartments. Weekly rates available.

DICTIONARY

adj adjective **adv** adverb **BE** British English **n** noun **prep** preposition **v** verb

A

a.m. del mattino
abbey l'abbazia
accept v accettare
access l'accesso
accident l'incidente
accommodation
  l'alloggio
account il conto
acupuncture
  l'agopuntura
adapter l'adattatore
address l'indirizzo
admission l'ingresso
after dopo; ~**noon** il
  pomeriggio; ~**shave**
  il dopobarba
age l'età
agency l'agenzia
AIDS l'AIDS
air l'aria; ~ **conditioning** l'aria condizionata; ~ **pump** la
  pompa dell'aria; ~**line**
  la compagnia aerea;
  ~**mail** la posta aerea;
  ~**plane** l'aereo;
  ~**port** l'aeroporto
aisle il corridoio; ~ **seat**
  il posto sul corridoio
allergic allergico; ~
  reaction la reazione
  allergica

allow v permettere
alone solo
alter v modificare
alternate route il
  percorso alternativo
aluminum foil la carta
  stagnola
amazing straordinario
ambulance
  l'ambulanza
American americano
amusement park il
  lunapark
and and
anemic anemico
anesthesia l'anestesia
animal l'animale
ankle la caviglia
antibiotic l'antibiotico
antiques store il
  negozio d'antiquariato
antiseptic cream la
  crema antisettica
anything qualsiasi
  cosa
apartment
  l'appartamento
appendix (body part)
  l'appendice
appetizer l'antipasto
appointment
  l'appuntamento
arcade la sala giochi

area code il prefisso
arm il braccio
aromatherapy
  l'aromaterapia
around (the corner)
  dietro di
arrivals (airport) gli
  arrivi
arrive v arrivare
artery l'arteria
arthritis l'artrite
art l'arte
aspirin l'aspirina
asthmatic asmatico
ATM il bancomat
attack l'aggressione
attend v frequentare
attraction (place)
  l'attrattiva
attractive attraente
Australia Australia
Australian australiano
automatic automatico;
  ~ **car** l'auto col
  cambio automatico
available libero

B

baby il bebè; ~ **bottle**
  il biberon; ~ **wipe** la
  salvietta per neonati;
  ~**sitter** la babysitter
back (body part) la

schiena; ~**ache** il
  mal di schiena;
  ~**pack** lo zaino
bag la borsa
baggage il bagaglio;
  ~ **claim** il ritiro
  bagagli; ~ **ticket** lo
  scontrino bagagli
bakery la panetteria
ballet lo spettacolo
  di danza
bandage la benda
bank la banca
bar il bar
barbecue il barbecue
barber il barbiere
baseball il baseball
basket (grocery store)
  il cestino
basketball il
  basketball
bathroom il bagno
battery la batteria
battleground il campo
  di battaglia
be v essere
beach la spiaggia
beautiful bello
bed il letto; ~
  and breakfast
  la pensione
begin v iniziare
before prima

beginner il principiante

behind dietro

beige beige

belt la cintura

berth la cuccetta

best il migliore

better migliore

bicycle la bicicletta

big grande

bigger più grande

bike route il percorso ciclabile

bikini il bikini; **~ wax** la ceretta all'inguine

bill v **(charge)** fatturare; **~** n **(money)** la banconota; **~** n **(of sale)** il conto

bird l'uccello

birthday il compleanno

black nero

bladder la vescica

bland insipido

blanket la coperta

bleed v sanguinare

blood il sangue; **~ pressure** la pressione sanguigna

blouse la camicetta

blue blu

board v imbarcarsi

boarding pass la carta d'imbarco

boat la barca

bone l'osso

book il libro; **~store** la libreria

boots gli stivali

boring noioso

botanical garden il giardino botanico

bother v infastidire

bottle la bottiglia; **~ opener** l'apribottiglie

bowl la coppa

box la scatola

boxing match l'incontro di boxe

boy il ragazzo; **~friend** il ragazzo

bra il reggiseno

bracelet il braccialetto

brakes (car) i freni

break v rompere; **~-in (burglary)** il furto con scasso; **~down** il guasto

breakfast la colazione

breast il petto; **~feed** v allattare

breathe v respirare

bridge il ponte

briefs (clothing) lo slip

bring v portare

British britannico(a)

broken rotto

brooch la spilla

broom la scopa

brother il fratello

brown marrone

bug l'insetto

building l'edificio

burn v bruciare

bus l'autobus; **~ station** la stazione degli autobus; **~ stop** la fermata del bus; **~ ticket** il biglietto del bus; **~ tour** l'escursione in pullman

business il lavoro; **~ card** il biglietto da visita; **~ center** il centro business; **~ class** la classe business; **~ hours** l'orario d'apertura

butcher il macellaio

buttocks le natiche

buy v comprare

bye ciao

C

cabaret il cabaret

cabin la cabina

cable car la funivia

cafe il caffè

call v chiamare; **~** n la chiamata

calories le calorie

camera la macchina fotografica; **digital ~** la macchina fotografica digitale; **~ case** l'astuccio della macchina fotografica; **~ store** il negozio di fotografia

camp v campeggiare; **~ stove** il fornello da campeggio; **~site** il campeggio

can opener l'apriscatole

Canada il Canada

Canadian canadese

cancel v annullare

candy le caramelle

canned good lo scatolame

canyon il canalone

car l'auto; **~ hire**

[BE] l'autonoleggio; **~ park [BE]** il parcheggio; **~ rental** l'autonoleggio; **~ seat** il seggiolino per auto

carafe la caraffa

card la carta; **ATM ~** il bancomat; **credit ~** la carta di credito; **debit ~** il bancomat; **phone ~** la scheda telefonica

carry on board v **[BE]** portare a bordo

carry-on il bagaglio a mano

cart (grocery store) il carrello; **~ (luggage)** il carrello

carton il cartone; **~ of cigarettes** la stecca di sigarette

case (container) la cassa

cash v incassare; **~** n i contanti; **~ advance** l'acconto

cashier il cassiere

casino il casinò

castle il castello

cathedral la cattedrale

cave la grotta

CD il CD

cell phone il telefonino

Celsius Celsius

centimeter il centimetro

certificate il certificato

chair la sedia; **~ lift** la seggiovia

change v **(buses)** cambiare; **~** v **(money)** cambiare; **~** v **(baby)** cambiare; **~** n **(money)** il cambio

charcoal il carbone

charge v **(credit card)** addebitare; **~** n **(cost)** il costo

cheap economico; **~er** più economico

check v **(on something)** controllare; **~** v **(luggage)** controllare; **~** n **(payment)** l'assegno; **~-in (hotel/airport)** il check-in; **~ing account** il conto corrente; **~ out (hotel)** il pagamento del conto

Cheers! Salute!

chemical toilet il WC da campeggio

chemist [BE] la farmacia

cheque [BE] l'assegno

chest (body part) il petto; **~ pain** il dolore al petto

chewing gum la gomma da masticare

child il bambino; **~ seat** il seggiolone; **~'s menu** il menù per bambino; **~'s portion** la porzione per bambino

Chinese cinese

chopsticks i bastoncini cinesi

church la chiesa

cigar il sigaro

cigarette la sigaretta

class la classe; **business ~** la classe business; **economy ~** la classe economica; **first ~** la prima classe

classical music la musica classica

clean v pulire; **~** adj pulito; **~ing product** il prodotto per la pulizia; **~ing supplies** i prodotti per la pulizia

clear v **(on an ATM)** cancellare

cliff la scogliera

cling film [BE] la pellicola per alimenti

close v **(a shop)** chiudere

close vicino

closed chiuso

clothing l'abbigliamento; **~ store** il negozio d'abbigliamento

club il club

coat il cappotto

coffee shop il caffè

coin la moneta

colander la scolapasta

cold (sickness) il raffreddore; **~ (temperature)** freddo

colleague il collega

cologne la colonia

color il colore

comb il pettine

come v venire

complaint il reclamo

computer il computer

concert il concerto; **~ hall** la sala da concerti

condition (medical) la condizione

conditioner il balsamo

condom il preservativo

conference la conferenza

confirm v confermare

congestion la congestione

connect v **(internet)** collegarsi

connection (internet) il collegamento; **~ (flight)** la coincidenza

constipated costipato

consulate il consolato

consultant il consulente

contact v contattare; **~ lens** la lente a contatto; **~ lens solution** la soluzione per lenti a contatto

contagious contagioso

convention hall la sala congressi

conveyor belt il nastro trasportatore

cook v cucinare

cooking gas il gas per cucina

cool (temperature) fresco

copper il rame

corkscrew il cavatappi

cost v costare

cot il lettino

cotton il cotone

cough v tossire; **~** n la tosse

country code il prefisso del paese

cover charge il coperto

crash v **(car)** fare un incidente

cream (ointment) la crema

credit card la carta di credito

crew neck a girocollo

crib la culla

crystal il cristallo

cup la tazza

currency la valuta; **~ exchange** il cambio valuta; **~ exchange office** l'ufficio di cambio

current account [BE] il conto corrente

customs la dogana

cut v **(hair)** tagliare; **~** n **(injury)** il taglio

cute carino

cycling il ciclismo

D

damage v danneggiare; **~d** danneggiato

dance v ballare; **~ club** il club di ballo; **~ing** il ballo

dangerous pericoloso
dark scuro
date (calendar) la data
day il giorno
deaf sordo
debit card il bancomat
deck chair la sedia a sdraio
declare v dichiarare
decline v (credit card) rifiutare
deeply profondamente
degrees (temperature) i gradi
delay v ritardare
delete v (computer) eliminare
delicatessen la gastronomia
delicious squisito
denim i jeans
dentist il dentista
denture la dentiera
deodorant il deodorante
department store il grande magazzino
departures (airport) le partenze
deposit v depositare; ~ (bank) n il deposito; ~ (to reserve a room) il deposito
desert il deserto
detergent il detersivo
develop v (film) sviluppare
diabetic diabetico
dial v comporre il numero
diamond il diamante

diaper il pannolino
diarrhea la diarrea
diesel il diesel
difficult difficile
digital digitale; ~ camera la macchina fotografica digitale; ~ photos le foto digitali; ~ prints le stampe digitali
dining room la sala da pranzo
dinner la cena
direction la direzione
dirty sporco
disabled il disabile; ~ accessible [BE] accessibile ai disabili
disconnect v (computer) scollegare
discount lo sconto
dish (kitchen) il piatto; ~washer la lavastoviglie; ~washing liquid il detersivo per i piatti
display lo schermo; ~ case la vetrinetta
disposable usa e getta; ~ razor la lametta usa e getta
dive v tuffarsi; ~ing equipment l'attrezzatura subacquea
divorce v divorziare
dizzy stordito

doctor il medico
doll la bambola
dollar (U.S.) il dollaro
domestic domestico; ~ flight il volo nazionale
door la porta
dormitory il dormitorio
double bed il letto matrimoniale
downtown (direction) il centro; ~ area il centro
dozen la dozzina
drag lift lo ski lift
dress (piece of clothing) il vestito; ~ code il codice di abbigliamento
drink v bere; ~ n la bevanda; ~ menu il menù delle bevande; ~ing water l'acqua potabile
drive v guidare
driver's license number il numero di patente
drop (medicine) la goccia
drowsiness la sonnolenza
dry cleaner il lavasecco
dubbed doppiato
during durante
duty (tax) la tassa; ~ free duty free
DVD il DVD

E

ear l'orecchio; ~ache il mal d'orecchio
earlier prima
early presto
earrings gli orecchini
east est
easy facile
eat v mangiare
economy class la classe economica
elbow il gomito
electric outlet la presa elettrica
elevator l'ascensore
e-mail v inviare e-mail; ~ n l'e-mail; ~ address l'indirizzo e-mail
emergency l'emergenza; ~ exit l'uscita d'emergenza
empty v svuotare
enamel (jewelry) lo smalto
end v finire
English inglese
engrave v incidere
enjoy v godersi
enter v entrare
entertainment l'intrattenimento
entrance l'entrata
envelope la busta
equipment l'attrezzatura
escalators le scale mobili
estate car [BE] la station wagon

e-ticket il biglietto elettronico

EU resident il residente UE

euro l'euro

evening la sera

excess l'eccesso

exchange v (money) cambiare; ~ n **(place)** il cambio; ~ **rate** il tasso di cambio

excursion l'escursione

excuse v scusare

exhausted esausto

exit v uscire; ~ n l'uscita

expensive caro

expert esperto

exposure (film) la posa

express espresso; ~ **bus** il bus espresso; ~ **train** il treno espresso

extension (phone) l'interno

extra extra; ~ **large** extra large

extract v **(tooth)** estrarre

eye l'occhio

eyebrow wax la ceretta per sopracciglie

F

face il viso

facial la pulizia del viso

family la famiglia

fan (appliance) il ventilatore; ~ **(sou-venir)** il ventaglio

far lontano; ~-**sighted** ipermetrope

farm la fattoria

fast veloce; ~ **food** il fast food

faster più veloce

fat free senza grassi

father il padre

fax v inviare per fax; ~ n il fax; ~ **number** il numero di fax

fee la tariffa

feed v dare da mangiare

ferry il traghetto

fever la febbre

field (sports) il campo

fill v riempire; ~ **out** v **(form)** compilare; ~**ing (tooth)** l'otturazione

film (camera) il rullino

fine (fee for breaking law) la multa

finger il dito; ~**nail** l'unghia

fire il fuoco; ~ **department** i vigili del fuoco; ~ **door** la porta antincendio

first primo; ~ **class** la prima classe

fit (clothing) v andare bene

fitting room il camerino

fix v **(repair)** riparare

flashlight la torcia elettrica

flat tire la gomma a terra

flight il volo

floor il pavimento

flower il fiore

folk music la musica folk

food il cibo

foot il piede

football game [BE] la partita di football

for per

forecast la previsione

forest il bosco

fork la forchetta

form il modulo

formula (baby) il latte in polvere

fort la fortezza

fountain la fontana

free libero

freezer il freezer

fresh fresco

friend l'amico

frying pan la padella

full-service il servizio completo

full-time a tempo pieno

G

game la partita

garage il garage

garbage bag il sacchetto per la spazzatura

gas (cooking) il gas per cucina; ~ **(heating)** il gas; ~ **station** la stazione del servizio; ~ **(vehicle)** la benzina

gate (airport) l'uscita

gay gay; ~ **bar** il bar per gay; ~ **club** il club per gay

gel (hair) il gel

get off v **(a train/bus/subway)** scendere

get to v arrivare

gift il regalo; ~ **shop** il negozio di articoli da regalo

girl la ragazza; ~**friend** la ragazza

give v dare

glass (drinking) il bicchiere; ~ **(material)** il vetro; ~**es** gli occhiali

go v **(somewhere)** andare

gold l'oro

golf golf; ~ **course** il campo da golf; ~ **club** la mazza; ~ **tournament** la gara di golf

good n il bene; ~ adj buono; ~ **afternoon** buon pomeriggio; ~ **evening** buonasera; ~ **morning** buongiorno; ~ **bye** arrivederla; ~**s** le merci

gram il grammo

grandchild il nipote

grandparent il nonno

gray grigio

green verde

grocery store il fruttivendolo

ground floor il pianterreno

**groundcloth [ground-
sheet BE]** il telone
impermeabile
group il gruppo
guide la guida; ~ **book**
la guida; ~ **dog** il
cane da guida
gym la palestra
gynecologist il
ginecologo

H

hair i capelli; ~ **dryer**
l'asciugacapelli; ~
salon il parruc-
chiere; ~**brush** la
spazzola ; ~ **cut** il
taglio; ~**spray** la
lacca; ~**style**
l'acconciatura; ~**styl-
ist** il parrucchiere
half la metà; ~ **hour**
la mezz'ora; ~~**kilo** il
mezzo chilo
hammer il martello
hand la mano; ~
luggage il bagaglio
a mano; ~**bag** la
borsetta
handicapped il disa-
bile; ~ **accessible**
accessibile ai disabili
hangover la sbornia
happy felice
hat il cappello
have v avere
head (body part) la
testa; ~**ache** il mal
di testa; ~**phones**
gli auricolari
health la salute;
~ **food store**

l'erboristeria
heart il cuore; ~
condition il disturbo
cardiaco
heat il calore; ~**er** il
radiatore
hello salve
helmet il casco
help v aiutare; ~ n
l'aiuto
here qui
heterosexual eter-
osessuale
hi ciao
high alto; ~**chair** il
seggiolone; ~**-heeled
shoes** le scarpe
col tacco alto; ~**way**
l'autostrada
hiking boots gli scarponi da montagna
hill la collina
hire v [BE] noleggiare;
~ **car [BE]** l'auto a
noleggio
hitchhike v fare
l'autostop
hockey l'hockey
holiday [BE] la
vacanza
horse track
l'ippodromo
hospital l'ospedale
hostel l'ostello
hot (temperature)
caldo; ~ **(spicy)**
piccante; ~ **springs**
le terme; ~ **water**
l'acqua calda
hotel l'hotel
hour l'ora
house la casa; ~**hold**

goods gli articoli
casalinghi; ~**keeping
services** i servizi di
pulizia domestica
how come; ~ **much**
quanto
hug v abbracciare
hungry affamato
hurt il dolore
husband il marito

I

ibuprofen l'ibuprofene
ice il ghiaccio; ~
hockey l'hockey su
ghiaccio
icy gelato
identification
l'identificazione
ill malato
in in
include v includere
indoor pool la piscina
interna
inexpensive a buon
mercato
infected infetto
information (phone)
le informazioni;
~ **desk** l'ufficio
informazioni
insect insetto; ~ **bite**
la puntura d'insetto;
~ **repellent** il repel-
lente per gli insetti
insert v inserire
insomnia l'insonnia
instant message il
messaggio istantaneo
insulin l'insulina
insurance
l'assicurazione;

~ **card** la tessera
dell'assicurazione;
~ **company** la
compagnia di as-
sicurazione
interesting interes-
sante
intermediate
intermedio
**international (airport
area)** internazi-
onale; ~ **flight** il
volo internazionale;
~ **student card** la
tessera internazionale
dello studente
internet l'Internet; ~
cafe l'Internet caffè;
~ **service** il servizio
Internet; **wireless
~** il collegamento
wireless a Internet
interpreter l'interprete
intersection l'incrocio
intestine l'intestino
introduce v presentare
invoice [BE] la fattura
Ireland l'Irlanda
Irish irlandese
iron v stirare; ~ n
(clothes) il ferro
da stiro
Italian italiano
Italy l'Italia

J

jacket la giacca
jar il vaso
jaw la mascella
jazz il jazz; ~ **club** il
club jazz
jeans i jeans

jet ski l'acquascooter
jeweler il gioielliere
jewelry la gioielleria
join v unire
joint (body part) la giuntura

K

key la chiave; **~ card** la chiave elettronica; **~ ring** il portachiavi
kiddie pool la piscina per bambini
kidney (body part) il rene
kilo il chilo; **~gram** il chilogrammo; **~meter** il chilometro
kiss v baciare
kitchen la cucina; **~ foil** la carta stagnola
knee il ginocchio
knife il coltello

L

lace il pizzo
lactose intolerant intollerante al lattosio
lake il lago
large grande
larger più grande
last ultimo
late (time) tardi
later più tardi
launderette [BE] la lavanderia a gettone
laundromat la lavanderia a gettone
laundry la lavanderia; **~ facility** il locale

lavanderia; **~ service** il servizio di lavanderia
lawyer l'avvocato
leather la pelle
leave v partire
left (direction) a sinistra
leg la gamba
lens la lente
less meno
lesson la lezione
letter la lettera
library la biblioteca
life la vita; **~ jacket** il giubbotto di salvataggio; **~guard** il bagnino
lift (ride) il passaggio; **~ [BE]** l'ascensore; **~ pass** il lift pass
light (overhead) la lampada; **~** v **(cigarette)** accendere; **~bulb** la lampadina; **~er** l'accendino
like v **(someone)** piacere
line (train) la linea
linen il lino
lip il labbro
liquor store l'enoteca
liter il litro
little piccolo
live v vivere
liver (body part) il fegato
loafers i mocassini
local locale
lock v chiudere; **~** n la serratura
locker l'armadietto

log off v **(computer)** fare il logoff
log on v **(computer)** fare il logon
long lungo; **~ sleeves** le maniche lunghe; **~-sighted [BE]** ipermetrope
look v guardare
lose v **(something)** perdere
lost perso; **~ and found** l'ufficio oggetti smarriti
lotion la lozione
louder più forte
love v **(someone)** amare; **~** n l'amore
low basso; **~er** più basso
luggage il bagaglio; **~ cart** il carrello bagagli; **~ locker** l'armadietto dei bagagli; **~ ticket** lo scontrino dei bagagli; **hand ~ [BE]** il bagaglio a mano
lunch il pranzo
lung il polmone

M

magazine la rivista
magnificent magnifico
mail v spedire; **~** n la posta; **~box** la cassetta della posta
main principale; **~ attraction** l'attrattiva principale; **~ course** il piatto principale
make up [BE] (a prescription) il trucco
mall il centro commerciale
man l'uomo
manager il responsabile
manicure il manicure
manual car l'auto col cambio manuale
map la cartina
market il mercato
married sposato
marry v sposare
mass (church service) la messa
massage il massaggio
match n **(wooden stick)** il fiammifero; **~** n **(game)** la partita
meal il pasto
measure v **(someone/something)** misurare; **~ing cup** la tazza di misurazione; **~ing spoon** il misurino
mechanic il meccanico
medicine la medicina
medium (size) medio
meet v **(someone)** incontrare
meeting (corporate) la riunione; **~ room** sala riunioni
membership card la tessera associativa
memorial (place) il monumento
memory card la scheda memoria

mend *v* riparare
menstrual cramp il crampo mestruale
menu il menù
message il messaggio
meter (parking) il parchimetro
microwave il microonde
midday [BE] mezzogiorno
midnight mezzanotte
mileage il chilometraggio
mini-bar il minibar
minute il minuto
missing (was never there) mancante; scomparso **(was previously there)**
mistake l'errore
mobile mobile; ~ **home** la casa prefabbricata; ~ **phone [BE]** il telefonino
mobility la mobilità
money il denaro
month il mese
mop lo spazzolone
moped lo scooter
more più
morning il mattino
mosque la moschea
mother la madre
motor il motore; ~ **boat** il motoscafo; ~**cycle** la motocicletta; ~**way [BE]** l'autostrada
mountain la montagna; ~ **bike** la mountain bike

mousse (hair) la mousse
mouth la bocca
movie il film; ~ **theater** il cinema
mug *v* scippare
muscle il muscolo
museum il museo
music la musica; ~ **store** il negozio di musica

N

nail l'unghia; ~ **file** la lima; ~ **salon** il salone di bellezza
name il nome
napkin il tovagliolo
nappy [BE] il pannolino
nationality la nazionalità
nature preserve la riserva naturale
(be) nauseous *v* avere la nausea
near vicino; ~**-sighted** miope
neck il collo; ~**lace** la collana
need *v* necessitare
newspaper il giornale
newsstand l'edicola
next prossimo
nice sympatico
night la notte; ~**club** il nightclub
no no
non-alcoholic analcolico
non-smoking non fumatori

noon mezzogiorno
north nord
nose il naso
notes [BE] le banconote
nothing niente
notify *v* avvertire
novice il principiante
now ora
number il numero
nurse l'infermiere

O

office l'ufficio; ~ **hours** l'orario d'ufficio
off-licence [BE] l'enoteca
oil l'olio
OK OK
old vecchio
on the corner all'angolo
once una volta
one uno; ~**-way (ticket)** solo andata; ~**-way street** il senso unico
only solo
open *v* aprire; ~ *adj* aperto
opera l'opera; ~ **house** il teatro dell'opera
opposite di fronte a
optician l'ottico
orange (color) arancione
orchestra l'orchestra
order *v* ordinare
outdoor pool la piscina esterna
outside fuori

over sopra; ~ **the counter (medication)** da banco; ~**look (scenic place)** il belvedere; ~**night** per la notte
oxygen treatment l'ossigeno terapia

P

p.m. del pomeriggio
pacifier il ciuccio
pack *v* fare le valigie
package il pacchetto
paddling pool [BE] la piscina per bambini
pad [BE] l'assorbente
pain il dolore
pajamas il pigiama
palace il palazzo
pants i pantaloni
pantyhose il collant
paper la carta; ~ **towel** la carta da cucina
paracetamol [BE] il paracetamolo
park *v* parcheggiare; ~ *n* il parco; ~**ing garage** il parcheggio; ~**ing lot** il parcheggio
parliament building l'edificio del parlamento
part (for car) il ricambio; ~ **time** part-time
pass through *v* passare
passenger il passeggero

passport il passaporto; **~ control** il controllo passaporti
password la password
pastry shop la pasticceria
path il sentiero
pay v pagare; **~ phone** il telefono pubblico
peak (of a mountain) la vetta
pearl la perla
pedestrian il pedone
pediatrician il pediatra
pedicure il pedicure
pen la penna
penicillin la penicillina
per per; **~ day** al giorno; **~ hour** all'ora; **~ night** a notte; **~ week** a settimana
perfume il profumo
period (menstrual) il ciclo; **~ (of time)** il periodo
permit v permettere
petite piccolo
petrol [BE] la benzina; **~ station [BE]** la stazione di servizio
pewter il peltro
pharmacy la farmacia
phone v telefonare; **~** n il telefono; **~ call** la telefonata; **~ card** la scheda telefonica; **~ number** il numero di telefono
photo la foto; **~copy**

la fotocopia; **~graphy** la fotografia
pick up v (something) raccogliere
picnic area la zona picnic
piece il pezzo
Pill (birth control) la pillola
pillow il cuscino
personal identification number (PIN) il codice PIN
pink rosa
piste [BE] la pista; **~ map [BE]** la cartina delle piste
pizzeria la pizzeria
place a bet v scommettere
plane l'aereo
plastic wrap la pellicola per alimenti
plate il piatto
platform (train) il binario
platinum il platino
play v giocare; **~** n (theater) lo spettacolo; **~ ground** il parco giochi; **~ pen** il box
please per favore
pleasure il piacere
plunger lo sturalavandini
plus size la taglia forte
pocket la tasca
poison il veleno
poles (skiing) le racchette

police la polizia; **~ report** il verbale di polizia; **~ station** il commissariato
pond lo stagno
pool (swimming) la piscina
pop music la musica pop
portion la porzione
post [BE] la posta; **~ office** l'ufficio postale; **~box [BE]** la buca delle lettere; **~card** la cartolina
pot (for cooking) la pentola, **~ (for flowers)** il vaso
pottery la ceramica
pounds (British sterling) le sterline
pregnant incinto
prescribe v prescrivere
prescription la ricetta
press v (clothing) stirare
price il prezzo
print v stampare
problem il problema
produce la frutta e verdura; **~ store** il fruttivendolo
prohibit v proibire
pronounce v pronunciare
public pubblico
pull v (door sign) tirare
purple viola
purse la borsetta
push v (door sign) spingere; **~chair**

[BE] il passeggino

Q

quality la qualità
question la domanda
quiet tranquillo

R

racetrack il circuito
racket (sports) la racchetta
railway station [BE] la stazione ferroviaria
rain la pioggia; **~coat** l'impermeabile; **~forest** la foresta pluviale; **~y** piovoso
rape v stuprare; **~** n lo stupro
rash l'irritazione
razor blade la lametta
reach v raggiungere
ready pronto
real vero
receipt la ricevuta
receive v ricevere
reception la reception
recharge v ricaricare
recommend v raccomandare
recommendation la raccomandazione
recycling il riciclaggio
red rosso
refrigerator il frigorifero
region la regione
registered mail la raccomandata
regular normale
relationship la relazione

rent v affittare
rental car l'auto a noleggio
repair v riparare
repeat v ripetere
reservation la prenotazione; **~ desk** l'ufficio prenotazioni
reserve v prenotare
restaurant il ristorante
restroom la toilette
retired in pensione
return v (something) portare indietro; **~** n [BE] la resa
rib (body part) la costola
right (direction) a destra; **~ of way** la precedenza
ring l'anello
river il fiume
road map la cartina stradale
rob v rubare; **~bed** derubato
romantic romantico
room la stanza; **~ key** la chiave della stanza; **~ service** il servizio in camera
round-trip l'andata e ritorno
route il percorso
rowboat la barca a remi
rubbish [BE] la spazzatura; **~ bag** [BE] il sacchetto per la spazzatura
rugby il rugby

ruins le rovine
rush la fretta

S

sad triste
safe (receptacle) la cassaforte; **~** (protected) sicuro
sales tax l'IVA
same stesso
sandals i sandali
sanitary napkin l'assorbente
saucepan la pentola
sauna la sauna
save v (computer) salvare
savings (account) i risparmi
scanner lo scanner
scarf la sciarpa
schedule v programmare; **~** n il programma
school la scuola
science la scienza
scissors le forbici
sea il mare
seat il posto
security la sicurezza
see v vedere
self-service il self-service
sell v vendere
seminar il seminario
send v inviare
senior citizen l'anziano
separated (marriage) separato
serious serio
service (in a restau-

rant) il servizio
sexually transmitted disease (STD) la malattia sessualmente trasmissibile
shampoo lo shampoo
sharp appuntito
shaving cream la crema da barba
sheet (bedlinen) il lenzuolo; **~** (paper) la pagina
ship v (mail) inviare
shirt la camicia
shoes le scarpe; **~ store** il negozio di calzature
shop v fare lo shopping
shopping lo shopping; **~ area** la zona commerciale; **~ centre** [BE] il centro commerciale; **~ mall** il centro commerciale
short corto; **~ sleeves** le maniche corte; **~s** i pantaloncini corti; **~-sighted** [BE] miope
shoulder la spalla
show v mostrare
shower la doccia
shrine il santuario
sick malato
side il lato; **~ dish** il contorno; **~ effect** l'effetto collaterale; **~ order** il contorno
sightseeing la visita turistica; **~ tour** la gita turistica

sign v firmare
silk la seta
silver l'argento
single (marriage) single; **~ bed** il letto a una piazza; **~ prints** le stampe singole; **~ room** la stanza singola
sink il lavandino
sister la sorella
sit v sedersi
size la taglia
skin la pelle
skirt la gonna
ski v sciare; **~** n lo sci; **~ lift** lo ski lift
sleep v dormire; **~er car** il vagone letto; **~ing bag** il sacco a pelo; **~ing car** [BE] il vagone letto
slice (of something) la fetta
slippers le ciabatte
slow lento; **~er** più lento; **~ly** lentamente
small piccolo; **~er** più piccolo
smoke v fumare
smoking (area) per fumatori
snack bar lo snack bar
sneakers le scarpe da ginnastica
snorkeling equipment l'attrezzatura da immersione
snow neve; **~board** lo snowboard; **~shoe** la scarpa da neve; **~y** nevoso

soap il sapone

soccer il calcio

sock il calzino

some qualche

soother [BE] il ciuccio

sore throat il mal
di gola

sorry scusi

south sud

souvenir il souvenir;
~ store il negozio di
souvenir

spa la stazione termale

spatula la spatola

speak v parlare

special (food) la specialità; **~ist (doctor)**
lo specialista

specimen il campione

speeding l'eccesso di
velocità

spell v scrivere

spicy piccante

spine (body part) la
spina dorsale

spoon il cucchiaio

sport lo sport; **~s
massage** il mas-
saggio sportivo

sporting goods store
il negozio di articoli
sportivi

sprain la storta

square quadrato;
**~ kilom-
eter** il chilometro
quadrato; **~ meter** il
metro quadrato

stadium lo stadio

stairs le scale

stamp v **(a
ticket)** convalidare;

~ n (postage) il
francobollo

start v iniziare

starter [BE] lo starter

station la stazione;
bus ~ la stazione dei
bus; **gas ~** il benzi-
naio; **petrol ~ [BE]**
il benzinaio; **railway
~ [BE]** la stazione
ferroviaria; **subway
~** la stazione della
metropolitana **train
~** la stazione ferro-
viaria; **underground
~ [BE]** la stazione
della metropolitana;
~ wagon la station
wagon

statue la statua

stay v stare

steal v rubare

steep ripido

sterling silver
l'argento massiccio

sting la puntura

stolen rubato

stomach lo stomaco;
~ache il mal di
stomaco

stop v fermarsi; **~** n la
fermata

store directory la
piantina del negozio

storey [BE] il piano

stove la cucina

straight dritto

strange strano

stream il ruscello

stroller il passeggino

student lo studente

study v studiare

stunning fenomenale

subtitle il sottotitolo

subway la metro-
politana; **~ station**
la stazione della
metropolitana

suit l'abito; **~case** la
valigia

sun il sole; **~block**
il filtro solare;
~burn la scot-
tatura; **~glasses**
gli occhiali da sole;
~ny soleggiato;
~screen il
filtro solare; **~stroke**
l'insolazione

super (fuel) la super;
~market il super-
mercato; **~vision**
la supervisione

surfboard la tavola
da surf

swallow v ingoiare

sweater il maglione

sweatshirt la felpa

sweet (taste) dolce;
~s [BE] le cara-
melle

swelling il gonfiore

swim v nuotare; **~suit**
il costume da bagno

symbol (keyboard) il
simbolo

synagogue la
sinagoga

T

table il tavolo

tablet (medicine) la
compressa

take v prendere; **~**

away [BE] portare
via

tampon il tampone

taste v assaggiare

taxi il taxi

team la squadra

teaspoon il cucchiaino

telephone il telefono

temple (religious) il
tempio

temporary provvisorio

tennis il tennis

tent la tenda; **~ peg**
il picchetto da tenda;
~ pole il paletto
da tenda

terminal (airport) il
terminal

terracotta la ter-
racotta

terrible terribile

text v **(send a mes-
sage)** inviare SMS;
~ n **(message)** il
testo

thank v ringraziare; **~
you** grazie

that che

theater il teatro

theft il furto

there là

thief il ladro

thirsty assetato

this questo

throat la gola

ticket il biglietto; **~
office** la bigliette-
ria; **~ed passenger**
il passeggero con
biglietto

tie (clothing) la
cravatta

time il tempo; **~table [BE]** l'orario

tire lo pneumatico

tired stanco

tissue il fazzoletto di carta

tobacconist il tabaccaio

today oggi

toe il dito del piede; **~nail** l'unghia

toilet [BE] la toilette; **~ paper** la carta igienica

tomorrow domani

tongue la lingua

tonight stanotte

too troppo

tooth il dente; **~paste** il dentifricio

total (amount) il totale

tough (food) duro

tourist il turista; **~ information office** l'ufficio informazioni turistiche

tour la gita

tow truck il carro attrezzi

towel l'asciugamano

tower la torre

town la città; **~ hall** il municipio; **~ map** la cartina della città; **~ square** la piazza della città

toy il giocattolo; **~ store** il negozio di giocattoli

track (train) il binario

traditional tradizionale

traffic light il semaforo

trail il sentiero; **~ map** la mappa dei sentieri

trailer la roulotte

train il treno; **~ station** la stazione ferroviaria

transfer v **(change trains/flights)** cambiare; **~** v **(money)** trasferire

translate v tradurre

trash la spazzatura

travel viaggiare; **~ agency** l'agenzia viaggi; **~ sickness (air)** il mal d'aria; **~ sickness (car)** il mal d'auto; **~ sickness (sea)** il mal di mare; **~ers**

tree l'albero

trim (hair) una spuntatina

trip il viaggio

trolley [BE] il carrello

trousers i pantaloni

T-shirt la maglietta

turn off v spegnere

turn on v accendere

TV la TV

type v battere a macchina

tyre [BE] lo pneumatico

U

United Kingdom (U.K.) il Regno Unito

United States (U.S.) gli Stati Uniti

ugly brutto

umbrella l'ombrello

unattended incustodito

unconscious inconscio

underground [BE] la metropolitana; **~ station [BE]** la stazione della metropolitana

underpants le mutande

understand v capire

underwear la biancheria intima

university l'università

unleaded (gas) senza piombo

upper superiore

upset stomach lo stomaco in disordine

urgent urgente

use v usare

username il nome utente

V

vacancy la disponibilità

vacation la vacanza

vaccination la vaccinazione

vacuum cleaner l'aspirapolvere

vaginal infection l'infezione vaginale

valid valido

valley la valle

valuable di valore

value il valore

VAT [BE] l'IVA

vegetarian vegetariano

vehicle registration il numero di targa

viewpoint la prospettiva

village il villaggio

vineyard il vigneto

visa il visto

visit v visitare; **~ing hours** gli orari di visita

visually impaired ipovedente

volleyball game la partita di pallavolo

vomit v vomitare

W

wait v attendere; **~** n l'attesa; **~ing room** la sala d'attesa

waiter il cameriere

waitress la cameriera

wake v svegliare, svegliarsi; **~-up call** il servizio sveglia

walk v camminare; **~** n la passeggiata; **~ing route** il percorso pedonale

wallet il portafogli

warm v **(something)** riscaldare; **~** adj **(temperature)** caldo

washing machine la lavatrice

watch l'orologio

water skis lo sci d'acqua

waterfall la cascata

weather il tempo

week la settimana;
~end il fine settimana; ~ly
settimanalmente
welcome v accogliere
west ovest
what (question) cosa
wheelchair la sedia a
rotelle; ~ ramp la
rampa per sedia a
rotelle
when (question)
quando
where (question)

dove
white bianco; ~ gold
l'oro bianco
who (question) chi
widowed vedovo
wife la moglie
window la finestra; ~
case la vetrina
windsurfer il windsurf
wine list la carta
dei vini
wireless wireless; ~
internet l'Internet
wireless; ~ internet

service il servizio
Internet wireless; ~
phone il telefono
cordless
with con
withdraw v
ritirare; ~al (bank)
il prelievo
without senza
woman la donna
wool la lana
work v lavorare
wrap v incartare
wrist il polso

write v scrivere

Y

year l'anno
yellow giallo; ~ gold
l'oro giallo
yes sì
yesterday ieri
young giovane
youth hostel l'ostello
della gioventù

Z

zoo lo zoo

ITALIAN–ENGLISH

A

a buon mercato
inexpensive
a destra right
(direction)
a girocollo crew neck
a notte per night
a settimana per week
a sinistra left
(direction)
a tempo pieno
full-time
l'abbazia abbey
l'abbigliamento
clothing
abbracciare to hug
l'abito suit
accendere v light
(cigarette); ~ v turn
on (lights)
l'accendino lighter
accessibile ai disabili
handicapped- [disa-

bled BE] accessible
l'accesso access
accettare v accept
accogliere v welcome
l'acconciatura
hairstyle
l'acconto cash
advance
l'acqua water; ~ calda
hot water; ~ potabile
drinking water;
~scooter jet ski
l'adattatore adapter
addebitare v charge
(credit card)
l'aereo airplane
l'aeroporto airport
affamato hungry
affittare v rent
[hire BE]
l'agenzia agency; ~
viaggi travel agency
l'aggressione attack

(on person)
l'agopuntura acu-
puncture
l'AIDS AIDS
aiutare to help
l'aiuto n help
al giorno per day
l'albero tree
all'angolo on the
corner
allattare breastfeed
allergico allergic
l'alloggio accom-
modation
all'ora per hour
alto high
amare v love (someone)
l'ambulanza am-
bulance
americano American
l'amico friend
l'amore n love
analcolico non-

alcoholic
andare v go (some-
where), ~ bene fit
(clothing)
l'andata e ritorno
round-trip
l'anello ring
anemico anemic
l'anestesia anesthesia
l'animale animal
l'anno year
annullare v cancel
l'antibiotico antibiotic
l'antipasto appetizer
[starter BE]
l'anziano senior citizen
aperto adj open
l'appartamento apart-
ment
l'appendice appendix
(body part)
l'appuntamento
appointment

appuntito sharp

l'apribottiglie bottle opener

aprire v open

l'apriscatole can opener

arancione orange (color)

l'argento silver; ~ **massiccio** sterling silver

l'aria condizionata air conditioning

l'armadietto locker; ~ **dei bagagli** luggage locker

l'aromaterapia aromatherapy

arrivare v arrive

arrivederla goodbye

gli arrivi arrivals (airport)

l'arte art

l'arteria artery

gli articoli casalinghi household goods

l'artrite arthritis

l'ascensore elevator

l'asciugacapelli hair dryer

l'asciugamano towel

asmatico asthmatic

l'aspirapolvere vacuum cleaner

l'aspirina aspirin

assaggiare v taste

l'assegno n check (payment) [cheque BE]

assetato thirsty

l'assicurazione insurance

l'assorbente sanitary

napkin [pad BE]

l'astuccio della macchina fotografica camera case

attendere v wait

l'attesa n wait

attraente attractive

l'attrattiva attraction (place); ~ **principale** main attraction

l'attrezzatura equipment; ~ **da immersione** snorkeling equipment; ~ **subacquea** diving equipment

gli auricolari headphones

Australia Australia

australiano Australian

l'auto car; **~bus** bus; ~ **con il cambio automatico** automatic car; ~ **con il cambio manuale** manual car; ~ **a noleggio** rental [hire BE] car

automatico automatic

l'autonoleggio car rental [hire BE]

l'autostrada highway [motorway BE]

avere v have; ~ **la nausea** v be nauseous

avvertire v notify

l'avvocato lawyer

B

la babysitter babysitter

baciare v kiss

il bagaglio luggage

[baggage BE]; ~ **a mano** carry-on [hand luggage BE]

il bagnino lifeguard

il bagno bathroom

ballare v dance

il ballo dancing

il balsamo conditioner

il bambino child

la bambola doll

la banca bank

il bancomat ATM, ATM card, debit card

la banconota n bill (money) [note BE]

il bar bar; ~ **per gay** gay bar

il barbecue barbecue

il barbiere barber

la barca boat; ~ **a remi** rowboat

il baseball baseball

il basketball basketball

basso low

i bastoncini cinesi chopsticks

battere a macchina v type

la batteria battery

il bebè baby

beige beige

bello beautiful

il belvedere overlook (scenic place)

ben riposato well-rested

la benda bandage

bene good

la benzina gas (vehicle) [petrol BE]

il benzinaio gas

[petrol BE] station

bere v drink

la bevanda n drink

la biancheria intima underwear

bianco white

il biberon baby bottle

la biblioteca library

il bicchiere glass (drinking)

la bicicletta bicycle

la biglietteria ticket office

il biglietto ticket; ~ **del bus** bus ticket; ~ **elettronico** e-ticket; ~ **da visita** business card

il bikini bikini

il binario platform; track (train)

blu blue

la bocca mouth

la borsa bag

la borsetta purse [handbag BE]

il bosco forest

la bottiglia bottle

il box playpen

il braccialetto bracelet

il braccio arm

bruciare v burn

brutto ugly

la buca delle lettere postbox

buongiorno good morning

buon pomeriggio good afternoon

buonasera good evening

buono *adj* good
il bus espresso
express bus
la busta envelope

C

il cabaret cabaret
la cabina cabin
il caffè cafe, coffee
il calcio soccer
caldo hot (temperature)
il calore heat (heating BE)
le calorie calories
il calzino sock
cambiare *v* change;
~ *v* exchange; ~
v transfer
il cambio *n* change
(money); ~
n exchange (place);
~ **valuta** currency
exchange
la cameriera waitress
il cameriere waiter
la camicetta blouse
la camicia shirt
camminare *v* walk
campeggiare *v* camp
il campeggio
campsite
il campione specimen
il campo field (sports);
~ **da golf** golf
course; ~ **di battaglia** battleground
il Canada Canada
canadese Canadian
il canalone canyon
cancellare *v* clear (on
an ATM)

il cane da guida
guide dog
i capelli hair
capire *v* understand
il cappello hat
il cappotto coat
la caraffa carafe
le caramelle candy
[sweet BE]
il carbone charcoal
carino cute
caro expensive
il carrello cart (trolley
BE); ~ **bagagli**
luggage cart
il carro attrezzi tow
truck
la carta card, paper;
~ **di credito** credit
card; ~ **da cucina**
paper towel; ~ **igienica** toilet paper;
~ **d'imbarco** boarding pass; ~ **stagnola**
aluminum [kitchen
BE] foil; ~ **dei vini**
wine list
la cartina map; ~
della città town
map; ~ **delle piste**
trail [piste BE] map;
~ **stradale** road
map
la cartolina postcard
il cartone carton
la casa house
la cascata waterfall
il casco helmet
il casinò casino
la cassa case (container); ~**forte** safe
(for valuables)

**la cassetta della
posta** mailbox
il cassiere cashier
il castello castle
la cattedrale
cathedral
il cavatappi corkscrew
la caviglia ankle
il CD CD
Celsius Celsius
la cena dinner
il centimetro
centimeter
il centro downtown
area; ~ **business**
business center;
~ **commerciale**
shopping mall
[centre BE]
la ceramica pottery
la ceretta wax; ~
all'inguine bikini
wax; ~ **per sopracciglie** eyebrow wax
il certificato
certificate
il cestino basket
(grocery store)
che that
il check-in check-in
(hotel/airport)
chi who
chiamare *v* call
la chiamata *n* call
la chiave key; ~
elettronica key
card; ~ **della stanza**
room key
la chiesa church
il chilo kilo; ~**grammo**
kilogram; ~**metraggio** mileage;

~**metro** kilometer;
~**metro quadrato**
square kilometer
chiudere *v* close (a
shop); ~ *v* lock
chiuso closed
le ciabatte slippers
ciao hi, bye
il cibo food
il ciclismo cycling
il ciclo period
(menstrual)
il cinema movie theater
cinese Chinese
la cintura belt
il circuito racetrack
la città town
il ciuccio pacifier
[soother BE]
la classe class; ~
business business
class, ~ **economica**
economy class
il club club; ~ **di ballo**
dance club; ~ **jazz**
jazz club; ~ **per gay**
gay club
il codice code;
~ **di abbigliamento**
dress code; ~ **PIN**
personal identification number (PIN)
la coincidenza connection (flight)
la colazione breakfast
la collana necklace
il collant pantyhose
il collega colleague
il collegamento connection (internet); ~
wireless a Internet
wireless internet

collegarsi v connect (internet)
la collina hill
il collo neck
la colonia cologne
il colore color
il coltello knife
come how
il commissariato police station
la compagnia aerea airline
la compagnia di assi-curazione insurance company
compilare v fill out (form)
il compleanno birthday
comporre il numero v dial
comprare v buy
la compressa tablet (medicine)
il computer computer
con with
il concerto concert
la condizione condi-tion (medical)
la conferenza confer-ence
confermare v confirm
la congestione congestion
il consolato consulate
il consulente consultant
contagioso contagious
i contanti n cash
contattare to contact
il conto n bill (of sale); ~ account; ~

corrente checking [current BE] account
il contorno side dish
controllare v check (luggage)
il controllo passaporti passport control
convalidare v stamp (a ticket)
la coperta blanket
il coperto cover charge
la coppa bowl
il corridoio aisle
corto short
cosa what (question)
la coscia thigh
costare v cost
costipato constipated
il costo charge (cost)
la costola rib (body part)
il costume da bagno swimsuit
il cotone cotton
il crampo mestruale menstrual cramp
la cravatta tie (clothing)
la crema cream (oint-ment); ~ **antisettica** antiseptic cream; ~ **da barba** shaving cream
il cristallo crystal
la cuccetta berth
il cucchiaino teaspoon
il cucchiaio spoon
la cucina kitchen, stove
cucinare v cook
la culla crib

il cuore heart
il cuscino pillow

D

da banco over the counter (medication)
danneggiare v damage
danneggiato damaged
dare v give; ~ **da mangiare** v feed
la data date (calendar)
del pomeriggio p.m.
il denaro money
il dente tooth
la dentiera denture
il dentifricio toothpaste
il dentista dentist
il deodorante deodorant
depositare v deposit
il deposito n deposit
derubato robbed
il deserto desert
il detersivo detergent; ~ **per i piatti** dishwashing liquid
di fronte a opposite
di valore valuable
diabetico diabetic
il diamante diamond
la diarrea diarrhea
dichiarare v declare
il diesel diesel
dietro around (the corner), behind (direction)
difficile difficult
digitale digital
la direzione direction
il disabile handi-capped [disabled BE]

la disponibilità vacancy
il disturbo cardiaco heart condition
il dito finger; ~ **del piede** toe
divorziare v divorce
la doccia shower
la dogana customs
dolce sweet (taste)
il dollaro dollar (U.S.)
il dolore hurt (pain); ~ **al petto** chest pain
la domanda question
domani tomorrow
domestico domestic
la donna woman
dopo after; ~**barba** aftershave
doppiato dubbed
dormire v sleep
il dormitorio dormitory
dove where (question)
la dozzina dozen
dritto straight
durante during
duro tough (food)
duty-free duty-free
il DVD DVD

E

e and
l'eccesso excess; ~ **di velocità** speeding
economico cheap
l'edicola newsstand
l'edificio building; ~ **del parlamento** parliament building
l'effetto collaterale side effect

eliminare v delete (computer)

l'e-mail n e-mail

l'emergenza emergency

l'enoteca liquor store [off-licence BE]

entrare v enter

l'entrata entrance

l'erboristeria health food store

l'errore mistake

esausto exhausted

l'escursione excursion; **~ in pullman** bus tour

esperto expert

espresso express

essere v be

est east

estrarre v extract (tooth)

l'età age

l'euro euro

extra extra; **~ large** extra large

F

facile easy

la famiglia family

fare v do; **~ l'autostop** v hitchhike; **~ la ceretta** v wax; **~ un incidente** v crash (car); **~ il logoff** v log off (computer); **~ il logon** v log on (computer); **~ lo shopping** v shop; **~ le valigie** v pack

la farmacia pharmacy

[chemist BE]

il fast food fast food

la fattoria farm

la fattura bill [invoice BE]

fatturare v bill (charge)

il fax n fax

il fazzoletto di carta tissue

la febbre fever

il fegato liver (body part)

felice happy

la felpa sweatshirt

fenomenale stunning

fermarsi v stop

la fermata n stop; **~ del bus** bus stop

il ferro da stiro n iron (clothes)

la fetta slice (of something)

il fiammifero n match (wooden stick)

il film movie

il filtro solare sunblock, sunscreen

il fine settimana weekend

la finestra window

finire v end

il fiore flower

firmare v sign

il fiume river

la fontana fountain

le forbici scissors

la forchetta fork

la foresta pluviale rainforest

il fornello da campeggio camping stove

la fortezza fort

la foto photo; **~ digitale** digital photo; **~copia** photocopy; **~grafia** photography

il francobollo n stamp (postage)

il fratello brother

freddo cold (temperature)

il freezer freezer

i freni brakes (car)

frequentare to attend

fresco cool (temperature); **~** fresh

la fretta rush

il frigorifero refrigerator

la frutta e verdura produce

il fruttivendolo grocery store

fumare v smoke

la funivia cable car

il fuoco fire

fuori outside

il furto theft; **~ con scasso** break-in (burglary)

G

la gamba leg

la gara di golf golf tournament

il garage garage

il gas gas (heating); **~ per cucina** cooking gas

la gastronomia delicatessen

gay gay

il gel gel (hair)

gelato icy

il ghiaccio ice

la giacca jacket

giallo yellow

il giardino botanico botanical garden

il ginecologo gynecologist

il ginocchio knee

giocare v play

il giocattolo toy

la gioielleria jewelry

il gioielliere jeweler

il giornale newspaper

il giorno day

giovane young

la gita tour; **~ turistica** sightseeing tour

il giubbotto di salvataggio life jacket

la giuntura joint (body part)

la goccia drop (medicine)

godersi v enjoy

la gola throat

il gomito elbow

la gomma rubber; **~ a terra** flat tire; **~ da masticare** chewing gum

il gonfiore swelling

la gonna skirt

i gradi degrees (temperature)

il grammo gram

grande big, large; **~ magazzino** department store

grazie thank you

grigio gray

la grotta cave
il gruppo group
guardare v look
il guasto breakdown
la guida guide, guide book
guidare v drive

H

l'hockey hockey; **~ su ghiaccio** ice hockey
l'hotel hotel

I

l'ibuprofene ibuprofen
l'identificazione identification
ieri yesterday
imbarcarsi v board
l'impermeabile raincoat
in in; **~ pensione** retired
incartare v wrap
incassare v cash
l'incidente accident
incidere v engrave
incinta pregnant
includere v include
inconscio unconscious
incontrare v meet (someone)
l'incontro di boxe boxing match
l'incrocio intersection
incustodito unattended
l'indirizzo address; **~ e-mail** e-mail address
infastidire v bother

l'infermiere nurse
infetto infected
l'infezione vaginale vaginal infection
le informazioni information (phone)
inglese English
ingoiare v swallow
l'ingresso admission
iniziare v begin, start
inserire v insert
l'insetto bug
insipido bland
l'insolazione sunstroke
l'insonnia insomnia
l'insulina insulin
interessante interesting
intermedio intermediate
internazionale international (airport area)
l'Internet internet; **~ caffè** internet cafe; **~ wireless** wireless internet
l'interno extension (phone)
l'interprete interpreter
l'intestino intestine
intollerante al lattosio lactose intolerant
l'intrattenimento entertainment
inviare v send, ship (mail); **~ e-mail** v e-mail; **~ per fax** v fax; **~ SMS** v text (send a message)

ipermetrope far- [long- BE] sighted
ipovedente visually impaired
l'ippodromo horsetrack
l'Irlanda Ireland
irlandese Irish
l'irritazione rash
l'Italia Italy
italiano Italian
l'IVA sales tax [VAT BE]

J

il jazz jazz
i jeans jeans

L

là there
la casa prefabbricata mobile home
la stanza singola single room
il labbro lip
la lacca hairspray
il ladro thief
il lago lake
la lametta razor blade; **~ usa e getta** disposable razor
la lampadina lightbulb
la lana wool
il latte in polvere formula (baby)
il lato side
la lavanderia laundry; **~ a gettone** laundromat [launderette BE]
il lavandino sink
il lavasecco dry

cleaner
la lavastoviglie dishwasher
la lavatrice washing machine
lavorare v work
il lavoro business
lentamente slowly
la lente lens; **~ a contatto** contact lens
il lenzuolo sheet
la lettera letter
il lettino cot
il letto bed; **~ matrimoniale** double bed; **~ a una piazza** single bed
la lezione lesson
libero available, free
la libreria bookstore
il libro book
il lift pass lift pass
la lima nail file
la linea line (train)
la lingua tongue
il lino linen
il litro liter
locale local
lontano far
la lozione lotion
la luce light (overhead)
il lunapark amusement park
lungo long

M

la macchina fotografica camera; **~ digitale** digital camera

il macellaio butcher
la madre mother
la maglietta T-shirt
il maglione sweater
magnifico magnificent
il mal sickness; ~
d'aria motion sickness (air); ~ **d'auto** motion sickness (car); ~ **di gola** sore throat; ~ **di mare** motion sickness (sea); ~ **d'orecchio** earache; ~ **di schiena** backache; ~ **di stomaco** stomachache; ~ **di testa** headache
malato sick [ill BE]
malattia sessualmente trasmissibile sexually transmitted disease (STD)
mancante missing
mangiare v eat
le maniche sleeves; ~ **corte** short sleeves; ~ **lunghe** long sleeves
il manicure manicure
la mano hand
il mare sea
il marito husband
marrone brown
il martello hammer
la mascella jaw
il massaggio massage; ~ **sportivo** sports massage
il mattino morning

del mattino a.m.
il meccanico mechanic
la medicina medicine
il medico doctor
medio medium (size)
meno less
il menù menu; ~ **delle bevande** drink menu; ~ **per bambini** children's menu
il mercato market
le merci goods
il mese month
la messa mass (church service)
il messaggio message; ~ **istantaneo** instant message
la metà half
il metro quadrato square meter
la metropolitana subway [underground BE]
la mezz'ora half hour
la mezzanotte midnight
il mezzo chilo half-kilo
mezzogiorno noon [midday BE]
il microonde microwave
migliore better
il migliore best
il minibar mini-bar
il minuto minute
miope near- [short-BE] sighted

misurare v measure (someone, something)
il misurino measuring spoon
mobile mobile
la mobilità mobility
i mocassini loafers
il mocio mop
modificare v alter (clothing)
il modulo form (fill-in)
la moglie wife
la moneta coin
la montagna mountain
il monumento memorial (place)
la moschea mosque
mostrare v show
la motocicletta motorcycle
il motore motor
il motoscafo motor boat
la mountain bike mountain bike
la mousse mousse (hair)
la multa fine (fee for breaking law)
il municipio town hall
il muscolo muscle
il museo museum
la musica music; ~ **classica** classical music; ~ **folk** folk music; ~ **pop** pop music
le mutande underpants

N

il naso nose
il nastro trasportatore conveyor belt
le natiche buttocks
la nazionalità nationality
necessitare v need
il negozio store; ~ **d'abbigliamento** clothing store; ~ **d'antiquariato** antique store; ~ **di articoli da regalo** gift shop; ~ **di articoli sportivi** sporting goods store; ~ **di calzature** shoe store; ~ **di fotografia** camera store; ~ **di giocattoli** toy store, ~ **di musica** music store; ~ **di souvenir** souvenir store
nero black
la neve snow
nevoso snowy
niente nothing
il nightclub nightclub
il nipote grandchild
no no
noioso boring
il nome name; ~ **utente** username
non fumatori non-smoking
il nonno grandparent
nord north
normale regular
la notte night

il numero number; **~ di fax** fax number; **~ di patente** driver's license number; **~ di targa** vehicle registration; **~ di telefono** phone number
nuotare v swim

O

gli occhiali glasses; **~ da sole** sunglasses
l'occhio eye
oggi today
OK OK
l'olio oil
l'ombrello umbrella
l'opera opera
ora now
l'ora hour
gli orari di visita visiting hours
l'orario schedule [timetable BE]; **~ d'apertura** business hours; **~ d'ufficio** office hours
l'orchestra orchestra
ordinare v order
gli orecchini earrings
l'orecchio ear
l'oro gold; **~bianco** white gold; **~ giallo** yellow gold
l'orologio watch; **~ da parete** wall clock
l'ospedale hospital
l'osso bone
l'ostello hostel; **~**

della gioventù youth hostel
l'ottico optician
l'otturazione filling (tooth)
ovest west

P

il pacchetto package
la padella frying pan
il padre father
il pagamento del conto check-out (hotel)
pagare v pay
il palazzo palace
la palestra gym
il paletto da tenda tent pole
la panetteria bakery
il pannolino diaper [nappy BE]
i pantaloncini corti shorts
i pantaloni pants [trousers BE]
il paracetamolo acetaminophen [paracetamol BE]
parcheggiare v park
il parcheggio parking garage; **~** parking lot [car park BE]
il parco n park; **~ giochi** playground
parlare v speak
il parrucchiere hair salon
le partenze departures (airport)
partire v leave
la partita game,

match; **~ di football** soccer [football game BE]; **~ di pallavolo** volleyball game
part-time part-time
il passaggio lift
il passaporto passport
passare v pass through
il passeggero passenger; **~ con biglietto** ticketed passenger
la passeggiata n walk
il passeggino stroller [pushchair BE]
la password password
la pasticceria pastry shop
il pasto meal
il pediatra pediatrician
il pedicure pedicure
il pedone pedestrian
la pelle leather, skin
la pellicola per alimenti plastic wrap [cling film BE]
il peltro pewter
il pene penis
la penicillina penicillin
la penna pen
la pensione bed and breakfast
la pentola saucepan, pot
per for, per; **~ favore** please; **~ fumatori** smoking (area); **~ la notte** overnight
il percorso route; **~ alternativo** alternate route;

~ ciclabile bike route; **~ pedonale** walking route
perdere v lose (something)
la perdita discharge (bodily fluid)
pericoloso dangerous
il periodo period (of time)
la perla pearl
permettere v allow, permit
perso lost
il pettine comb
il petto chest (body part)
il petto breast
il pezzo piece
piacere v like
il piacere pleasure
il piano floor [storey BE]
il pianterreno ground floor
la piantina del negozio store directory
il piatto plate; **~ principale** main course
la piazza della città town square
piccante hot (spicy)
il picchetto da tenda tent peg
piccolo little, petite, small
il piede foot
il pigiama pajamas
la pillola Pill (birth control)

la pioggia rain

piovoso rainy

la piscina pool; **~ per bambini** kiddie [paddling BE] pool; **~ esterna** outdoor pool; **~ interna** indoor pool

pista piste [BE]

più more; **~ basso** lower; **~ economico** cheaper; **~ forte** louder; **~ grande** bigger; **~ lento** slower; **~ piccolo** smaller; **~ tardi** later; **~ veloce** faster

la pizzeria pizzeria

il pizzo lace

il platino platinum

lo pneumatico tire [tyre BE]

la polizia police

il polmone lung

il polso wrist

il pomeriggio afternoon

la pompa dell'aria air pump

il ponte bridge

la porta door; **~ antincendio** fire door

il portachiavi key ring

il portafogli wallet

portare v bring; **~ indietro** v return (something); **~ via** to go [take away BE]

la porzione portion; **~ per bambini** children's portion

la posa exposure (film)

la posta n mail [post BE]; **~ aerea** airmail

il posto seat; **~ sul corridoio** aisle seat

il pranzo lunch

la precedenza right of way

il prefisso area code; **~ del paese** country code

il prelievo withdrawal (bank)

prendere v take

prenotare v reserve

la prenotazione reservation

la presa elettrica electric outlet

prescrivere v prescribe

presentare v introduce

il preservativo condom

la pressione sanguigna blood pressure

presto early

la previsione forecast

il prezzo price

prima before, earlier; **~ classe** first class

primo first

il principiante beginner, novice

il problema problem

i prodotti per la pulizia cleaning supplies

profondamente deeply

il profumo perfume

il programma n

schedule

programmare v schedule

proibire v prohibit

pronto ready

pronunciare v pronounce

la prospettiva viewpoint

prossimo next

provvisorio temporary

pubblico public

pulire v clean

pulito adj clean

la pulizia del viso facial

la puntura sting; **~ d'insetto** insect bite

Q

quadrato square

qualche some

la qualità quality

qualsiasi cosa anything

quando when (question)

quanto how much (question)

questo this

qui here

R

la racchetta racket (sports)

le racchette poles (skiing)

raccogliere v pick up (something)

raccomandare v recommend

la raccomandata

registered mail

la raccomandazione recommendation

il radiatore heater

il raffreddore cold (sickness)

la ragazza girl, girlfriend

il ragazzo boy, boyfriend

raggiungere v reach (get hold of)

il rame copper

la rampa per sedia a rotelle wheelchair ramp

il rap rap (music)

la reazione allergica allergic reaction

la reception reception

il reclamo complaint

il regalo gift

il reggiseno bra

la regione region

il Regno Unito United Kingdom (U.K.)

la relazione relationship

il rene kidney (body part)

il repellente per gli insetti insect repellent

il residente UE EU resident

respirare v breathe

il ricambio part (for car)

il riciclaggio n recycling

la ricetta prescription

ricevere v receive

la ricevuta receipt
il riciclaggio n
  recycling
riempire v fill
rifiutare v decline
  (credit card)
ringraziare v thank
riparare v fix, mend,
  repair
ripetere v repeat
ripido steep
il responsabile
  manager
il riscaldamento
  heating
riscaldare v warm
  (something)
la riserva naturale
  nature preserve
i risparmi savings
  (account)
il ristorante res-
  taurant
ritardare v delay
ritirare v withdraw
il ritiro bagagli bag-
  gage claim
la riunione meeting
la rivista magazine
romantico romantic
rompere v break
rosa pink
rosso red
rotto broken
la roulotte trailer
le rovine ruins
rubare v rob, steal
rubato stolen
il rugby rugby
il rullino film
  (camera)
il ruscello stream

S

il sacchetto per i
  rifiuti garbage
  [rubbish BE] bag
il sacco a pelo sleep-
  ing bag
la sala room; ~
  congressi conven-
  tion hall; ~ d'attesa
  waiting room; ~ da
  concerti concert
  hall; ~ da pranzo
  dining room; ~ giochi
  arcade; ~ riunioni
  meeting room
il salone di bellezza
  nail salon
la salute health
Salute! Cheers!
salvare v save
  (computer)
salve hello
la salvietta per
  neonati baby wipe
i sandali sandals
il sangue blood
sanguinare v bleed
il santuario shrine
il sapone soap
la sauna sauna
la sbornia hangover
le scale stairs; ~
  mobili escalators
lo scanner scanner
le scarpe shoes;
  ~ da neve snow-
  shoes; ~ basse flat
  shoes; ~ col tacco
  alto high-heeled
  shoes; ~ da gin-
  nastica sneakers
gli scarponi da

montagna hiking
  boots
la scatola box
lo scatolame canned
  good
scendere v get off (a
  train, bus, subway)
la scheda card; ~
  memoria memory
  card; ~ telefonica
  phone card
lo schermo display
la schiena back (body
  part)
lo sci n ski; ~ d'acqua
  water skis
sciare v ski
la sciarpa scarf
la scienza science
scippare v mug
la scogliera cliff
la scolapasta
  colander
scollegare v discon-
  nect (computer)
lo scollo a V V-neck
scommettere v place
  a bet
scomparso missing
lo sconto discount
lo scontrino bagagli
  luggage [baggage
  BE] ticket
lo scooter moped
la scopa broom
la scottatura sunburn
scrivere v spell, write
la scuola school
scuro dark
scusare v excuse
scusi sorry (apology)
sedersi v sit

la sedia chair; ~ a ro-
  telle wheelchair;
  ~ a sdraio deck
  chair
il sedile per bambino
  child's seat
il seggiolino per auto
  car seat
il seggiolone
  highchair
la seggiovia chair lift
il self-service self-
  service
il semaforo traffic light
il seminario seminar
il senso unico one-
  way street
senza without; ~
  grassi fat free; ~
  piombo unleaded
  (gas)
separato separated
  (marriage)
la sera evening
serio serious
la serratura n lock
I servizi di pulizia
  domestica house-
  keeping services
il servizio service (in a
  restaurant); ~ com-
  pleto full-service;
  ~ di lavanderia
  laundry service; ~
  in camera room
  service; ~ Internet
  internet service; ~
  Internet wireless
  wireless internet
  service; ~ sveglia
  wake-up call

la seta silk
la settimana week
settimanalmente weekly
lo shampoo shampoo
lo shopping shopping
sì yes
la sicurezza security
sicuro safe (protected)
la sigaretta cigarette
il sigaro cigar
il simbolo symbol (keyboard)
la sinagoga synagogue
single single (marriage)
lo ski lift drag lift, ski lift
lo slip briefs (clothing)
lo smalto enamel (jewelry)
lo snack bar snack bar
lo snowboard snowboard
il sole sun
soleggiato sunny
solo alone, only; **~ andata** one-way (ticket)
la soluzione per lenti a contatto contact lens solution
la sonnolenza drowsiness
sopra over
sordo deaf
la sorella sister
il sottotitolo subtitle
il souvenir souvenir
la spalla shoulder
la spatola spatula
la spazzatura trash

[rubbish BE]
la spazzola hairbrush
lo specialista specialist (doctor)
la specialità special (food)
spedire v mail
spegnere v turn off (lights)
lo spettacolo n play (theater); **~ di danza** ballet
la spiaggia beach
la spilla brooch
la spina dorsale spine (body part)
spingere v push (door sign)
lo spogliatoio fitting room
sporco dirty
lo sport sport
sposare v marry
sposato married
la spuntatina trim (hair)
la squadra team
squisito delicious
lo stadio stadium
lo stagno pond
stampare v print
la stampa n print; **~ digitale** digital print; **~ singola** single print
stanco tired
stanotte tonight
la stanza room
stare v stay
gli Stati Uniti United States (U.S.)
la station wagon

station wagon [estate car BE]
la statua statue
la stazione station; **~ degli autobus** bus station; **~ dei bus** bus station; **~ ferroviaria** train station [railway station BE]; **~ della metropolitana** subway station [underground station BE]; **~ di servizio** gas station [petrol station BE]; **~ termale** spa
la stecca di sigarette carton of cigarettes
le sterline pounds (British sterling)
stesso same
stirare v iron, press (clothing)
gli stivali boots
lo stomaco stomach; **~ in disordine** upset stomach
stordito dizzy
la storta sprain
strano strange
straordinario amazing
lo studente student
studiare v study
stuprare v rape
lo stupro n rape
lo sturalavandini plunger
sud south
la super super (fuel)
superiore upper
il supermercato supermarket
la supervisione

supervision
svegliare, svegliarsi v wake
sviluppare v develop (film)
svuotare v empty

T
il tabaccaio tobacconist
la taglia size; **~ forte** plus size
tagliare v cut (hair)
il taglio n cut (injury), haircut
il tampone tampon
tardi late (time)
la tariffa fee
la tasca pocket
la tassa duty (tax)
il tasso di cambio exchange rate
la tavola da surf surfboard
il tavolo table
il taxi taxi
la tazza cup; **~ di misurazione** measuring cup
il teatro theater; **~ dell'opera** opera house
telefonare v phone
la telefonata phone call
il telefonino cell [mobile BE] phone
il telefono n phone; **~** telephone; **~ cordless** wireless phone; **~ pubblico** pay phone

il telone impermeabile groundcloth [groundsheet BE]
il tempio temple (religious)
il tempo time, weather
la tenda tent
il tennis tennis
la terapia ad ossigeno oxygen treatment
le terme hot spring
il terminal terminal (airport)
la terracotta terracotta
terribile terrible
la tessera card; **~ associativa** membership card; **~ dell'assicurazione** insurance card; **~ internazionale dello studente** international student card
la testa head (body part)
il testo n text (message)
tirare v pull (door sign)
la toilette restroom [toilet BE]
la torcia elettrica flashlight
la torre tower
la tosse n cough
tossire v cough
il totale total (amount)
il tovagliolo napkin
tradizionale traditional
tradurre v translate

il traghetto ferry
tranquillo quiet
trasferire v transfer (money)
il travellers cheque travelers check [travelers cheque BE]
il treno train; **~ espresso** express train
triste sad
troppo too
tuffarsi v dive
il turista tourist
la TV TV

U

l'uccello bird
l'ufficio office; **~ di cambio** currency exchange office; **~ informazioni** information desk; **~ informazioni turistiche** tourist information office; **~ oggetti smarriti** lost and found; **~ postale** post office; **~ prenotazioni** reservation desk
ultimo last
una volta once
l'unghia fingernail, toenail
unire v join
l'università university
uno one
l'uomo man
urgente urgent
usa e getta disposable
usare v use

uscire v exit
l'uscita gate (airport), exit; **~ d'emergenza** emergency exit
l'utensile utensil

V

la vacanza vacation [holiday BE]
la vaccinazione vaccination
la vagina vagina
il vagone letto sleeper [sleeping BE] car
valido valid
la valigia suitcase
la valle valley
il valore value
la valuta currency
il vaso jar
vecchio old
vedere v see
vedovo widowed
vegetariano vegetarian
il veleno poison
veloce fast
vendere v sell
venire v come
il ventaglio fan (souvenir)
il ventilatore fan (appliance)
il verbale di polizia police report
verde green
vero real
la vescica bladder
il vestito dress (piece of clothing)
la vetrina window

case
la vetrinetta display case
il vetro glass (material)
la vetta peak (of a mountain)
il viaggio trip
vicino close, near, nearby, next to
i vigili del fuoco fire department
il vigneto vineyard
il villaggio village
viola purple
la visita turistica sightseeing
visitare v visit
il viso face
il visto visa
la vita life
la vitamina vitamin
vivere v live
il volo flight; **~ internazionale** international flight; **~ nazionale** domestic flight
vomitare v vomit

W

il WC da campeggio chemical toilet
il windsurf windsurfer

Z

lo zaino backpack
la zona area; **~ commerciale** shopping area; **~ picnic** picnic area
lo zoo zoo

INDEX

pocket guide

BOLOGNA

Second Edition 2019

Managing Editor: Carine Tracanelli
Author: Susie Boulton
Head of DTP and Pre-Press: Rebeka Davies
Picture Editor: Tom Smyth
Cartography Update: Carte
Update Production: Apa Digital
Photography Credits: Alamy 4ML, 14, 16, 26, 39, 53, 65, 70, 86, 91, 92, 94, 97, 102; Getty Images 1, 5MC, 5MC, 6L, 7, 17, 18, 20, 22, 25, 28, 32, 41, 47, 51, 56, 60, 75, 84, 98; iStock 4TC, 5T, 5TC, 5M, 81, 82; Shutterstock 4MC, 4TL, 5M, 6R, 7R, 11, 13, 31, 35, 36, 42, 44, 48, 54, 59, 67, 69, 73, 76, 79; SuperStock 88, 101, 105
Cover Picture: Henryk Sadura / Picfair

Distribution

UK, Ireland and Europe: Apa Publications (UK) Ltd; sales@insightguides.com
United States and Canada: Ingram Publisher Services; ips@ingramcontent.com
Australia and New Zealand: Woodslane; info@woodslane.com.au
Southeast Asia: Apa Publications (SN) Pte; singaporeoffice@insightguides.com
Worldwide: Apa Publications (UK) Ltd; sales@insightguides.com

Special Sales, Content Licensing and CoPublishing
Insight Guides can be purchased in bulk quantities at discounted prices. We can create special editions, personalised jackets and corporate imprints tailored to your needs. sales@insightguides.com; www.insightguides.biz

Contact us
Every effort has been made to provide accurate information in this publication, but changes are inevitable. The publisher cannot be responsible for any resulting loss, inconvenience or injury. We would appreciate it if readers would call our attention to any errors or outdated information. We also welcome your suggestions; please contact us at: berlitz@apaguide.co.uk
www.insightguides.com/berlitz